all woman

BUMPER

© 2007 by Faber Music Ltd
First published by Faber Music Ltd in 2007
Bloomsbury House 74–77 Great Russell Street London WC1B 3DA
Edited by Beth Millett & Lucy Holliday
Compiled by Lucy Holliday
Engraved by Kasia Middleton
Printed in England by Caligraving Ltd

ISBN10: 0-571-52761-2
EAN13: 978-0-571-52761-8

To buy Faber Music publications or to find out about the full range of titles available,
please contact your local music retailer, or Faber Music sales enquiries:

Faber Music Ltd, Burnt Mill, Elizabeth Way, Harlow, CM20 2HX England
Tel: +44 (0) 1279 82 89 82   Tel: +44 (0) 1279 82 89 83
sales@fabermusic.com   fabermusic.com

all woman
BUMPER

ALL WOMAN

Words and Music by Lisa Stansfield, Ian Devaney and Andy Morris

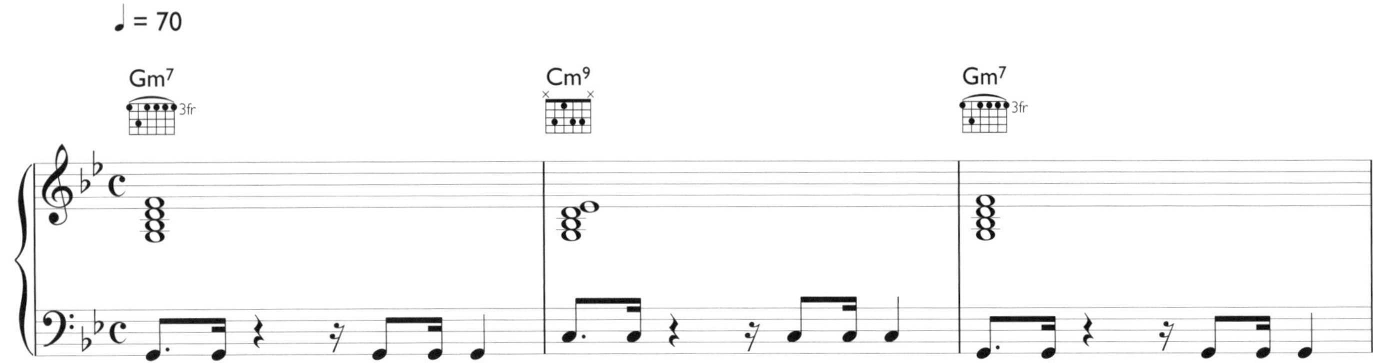

Cm9
Gm7 3fr
C/E
be O. K.   it's hard for her when he does-n't res - pond.____   He says
the lov-ing go?   The love they used to share when they were strong.____   She says
-ing for his pay.   He has-n't seen the pain he's put her through.____   At -ten-

E♭maj7
Gm7 3fr
C
babe you look a mess,   you look dow-dy in that dress,   it's just not like it used to be,
yes, I look a mess,   but I don't love you any less   I thought you always thought enough of me,
-tion that he paid____   just van-ished in the haze,___   he re - mem-bers how it used to be

C/D
E♭maj7
Dm7
Daug7
then she says____   but I'm all wo-man,
to always be im-pressed   I may not be a la-dy
when he used to say,   You'll al-ways be a la-dy   'cause you're all wo-man,

Cm7
F/G
G7
Ebmaj7
from Mon - day to Sun - day
I work hard - er than you know.
I work my fingers to the bone.
from Mon - day to Sun - day I love you much more than you know.
I'm no clas - sy la - dy,
You're a clas - sy la - dy,

Dm7
C9
Cm7
F/G
G7
but I'm all wo - man,
and this wo - man needs a lit - tle love to make her strong.
This wo - man needs a lit - tle love to make her strong.
'cause you're all wo - man. This wo - man needs a lov - ing man to keep her warm.

Ebmaj7
Bbmaj7
Ebmaj7
You're not the on - ly one.

To Coda
D.S. al Coda
Coda
repeat ad lib. to fade out
2.She
3.He
Ooh you're a clas - sy la - dy 'cause you're
So sweet the love that used to be.
all So sweet the love that used to be.
wo - man.
We can be sweet a - gain.

BEWITCHED

Words and Music by Richard Rodgers and Lorenz Hart

= 77
C11 Am7 Gm7 F Dm7 Gm B♭/C F Faug
blink._____ I'm wild a-gain, be - guiled a - gain, a sim-per-ing,_ whim - per-ing
B♭ Bdim F/C Ddim Gm7/C C7 D7♭9 Gm Gm(maj7)
child a-gain. Be-witched, both-ered_ and be - wil-dered am I._______________
Gm7 C7 F Dm7 Gm7 B♭/C C7 F Faug
Could-n't sleep and_ would-n't sleep, when love_ came and told me
B♭ Bdim F/C Ddim Gm7/C C7 Cm7 F7 B♭maj7
I should-n't sleep. Be - witched, both-ered and be-wil-dered_ am I._______________

Am7 D Gm Gm(maj7) Gm7 Gm6 Dm Dm(maj7)
Lost my heart, but what of it. He is cold____ I a-
Dm7 Dm6 B♭maj7 Am7 Gm7 Gm7/C C7 A7 A♭dim
-gree. He can laugh, but I love it,__ al-though the laugh's on
Gm7 C13 F Dm7 G7 C11 C7 F Faug
me.________ I'll sing to him, each spring to him, and long for the day__ when I'll_
B♭ Bdim F/C Ddim Gm7/C C7 F
_ cling to him.__ Be-witched, both-ered__ and be-wil-dered am I.________

Rubato
F/A   D♭/A♭   Gm7   C13   Fmaj9   Dm7   Gm7   C7♭9
He's a fool and don't I know it, but a fool can
Fmaj7   D7♭9   Gm7   C7   Fmaj7   Dm7   Gm7   C7
have his charms. I'm in love and don't I show it, like a babe in arms.
Fmaj7   Dm   Gm7   C13   Fmaj7   Dm   Gm   C13
Love's the same old sad sen-sa-tion, late-ly I've not
rit.
Fmaj9   D7♭9   Gm7   C13   Fmaj9   Dm11   Gm7
slept a wink. Since this half-pint im-i-ta-tion put me on the blink.

a tempo (♩ = 77)
I've sinned a lot, I___ mean a lot, but I'm___ like sweet sev - en -
- teen a lot. Be - witched, both - ered and be - wil - dered am I.___
I'll sing to him, each spring to him, and wor - ship the trou - sers that cling
to him.___ Be - witched, both - ered and be - wil - dered am I.___

Am7 D7 Gm Gm(maj7) Gm7 Gm6 Dm Dm(maj7)
When he talks_ he is seek- ing_ words_ to get off his
Dm7 Dm6 B♭maj7 Am7 Gm7 B♭/C C7 Am7 A♭dim
chest. Ho - ri - zon - tal- ly speak - ing_ he's at his ve - - ry
Gm7 C13 F Dm7 Gm Gm7/C C7 F Faug
best._ Vexed a - gain, per- plexed a - gain. Thank God I can be_ o - ver
B♭ Bdim F/C Ddim Gm7/C C7 F Dm7
- sexed a - gain._ Be - witched, both - ered and be - wil - dered am I._

Gm7 Gm7/C C7 F Dm7 Gm7 G♭maj7 F Faug
Wise at last, my eyes___ at last are cut-ting you down___ to your

B♭6 Bdim Bdim/E F Bm7♭5 Bdim/E Am7♭5 D7♭9 Gm Gm(maj7)
size at last. Be - witched, both - ered and be-wil-dered no more___

Gm7 C F Dm7 Gm7 G♭maj7 F Faug
Burned a lot but learned a lot and now you are broke___ so you

B♭ Bdim Bdim/E F Ddim Gm7/C C7 Cm7 F7 B♭maj7
earned a lot. Be - witched, both - ered and___ be-wil-dered___ no more___

Would-n't eat,__ was__ dys-pep-tic. Life__was so__ hard
to bear. Now my heart's an - ti-sep-tic,__ since you moved out of
there________ Ro - mance fi-nis,__ your chance fi - nis.__ Those ants that in - vad-ed my pants
________ fi - nis.__ Be - witched, both-ered__ and be - wil-dered no more.____________
rall.

BLACK VELVET

Words and Music by Christopher Ward and David Tyson

15
ba - by___ on her shoul - der,   the sun is set - tin' like_ mo - las - ses__ in the sky.___
heart of___ ev - 'ry school girl,   "Love Me Ten - der" leaves 'em cry - in'___ in the aisle.___
Bb7sus4   Bb7   Ab7sus4   Ab7   Gb7sus4   Gb7
18
The boy could sing; knew how to move   ev - 'ry - thing,___   al - ways want - ing more,
The way he moved it was___   a sin, so sweet and true.___
Dbsus4   Abm7   Db
21
he'll leave you long - ing for_   black vel - vet and that   lit - tle boy_ smile,_
Abm7   Fb   Cb   Abm7
24
black vel - vet {with} {and} that slow south - ern style.   A new re - li - gion___ that - 'll

18
27
D♭
4fr
bring you___ to your knees,
1.
C♭7
7fr
B♭7sus4
6fr
E♭5
6fr
black vel - vet,___ if you please.
30
2.
C♭7
7fr
B♭7sus4
6fr
E♭m7
6fr
33
black vel - vet,___ if you please.
A♭m
4fr
B♭7
6fr
E♭m7
6fr
36
Ev-'ry word_ of ev-'ry song_ that he sang_ was for you.___

19
39
A♭m
F♭
In a flash he was gone,___ it hap-pened so
42
C♭
B♭7
E♭m7
soon.___ What could you___ do?___
(Guitar solo)
46
51
A♭m7
D♭
A♭m7
Black vel - vet and that lit-tle boy_ smile, black vel - vet in that

slow south-ern style.
A new re-li-gion_ that-'ll bring you___ to your knees,
black vel-vet,
if you please.___
black vel-vet,
if__ you_
please,___
if you
please.___
(Fade begins)
Fade out

CAN'T FIGHT THE MOONLIGHT

Words and Music by Diane Warren

A
Em7
un - til 'til the sun goes down.
too long 'til you're in my arms.
Un - der - neath the star-
Un - der - neath the star-
D
Em7
D/F#
- light, star - light, there's a mag - i - cal feel - ing so right.
- light, star - light, we'll be lost in a rhy - thm so right.
G
G5
N.C.
Cm
It will steal your heart to - night.
Feel it steal your heart to - night.
You can try to re - sist, try to hide
Fm7
Bb
Ab
G
from my kiss but you know, but you know that you can't fight the moon - light. Deep

Cm   Fm7   Bb
in the dark, you'll sur - ren - der your heart. But you know, don't you know that you
Ab   G   Fm7   G7
can't fight the moon - light, no, you can't fight it. It's
G/B   G7   Fm7
gon - na get to your heart. it. No mat - ter what
G7   N.C.   Bm7
you do the night is gon - na get to you.
1.
2.

Em7
A
Can't fight__ it.__ Don't try__ it, you're ne - ver gon - na win,_ cos,__
Fm7
Eb
Fm7
un - der - neath__ the star - light, star - light,__ there's a mag - i - cal feel-
Eb/G
Ab
Ab5
- ing so__ right. It will steal_ your heart__ to - night.__ You can try__
C#m
F#m7
B
__ to re - sist,_ try to hide__ from my kiss__ but you know,___ but you know_ that you

46
A
G#
C#m
F#m7
can't fight the moon - light. Deep___ in the dark,_ you'll sur - ren - der your heart._ But you know,

49
B
A
G#
F#m7
___ but you know_ that you   can't fight the moon - light, no,____   you can't fight

1.
2.
G#7
G#7
52
it.   You can try___ it.   It's gon - na get to your heart.________

CABARET

Words by Fred Ebb
Music by John Kander

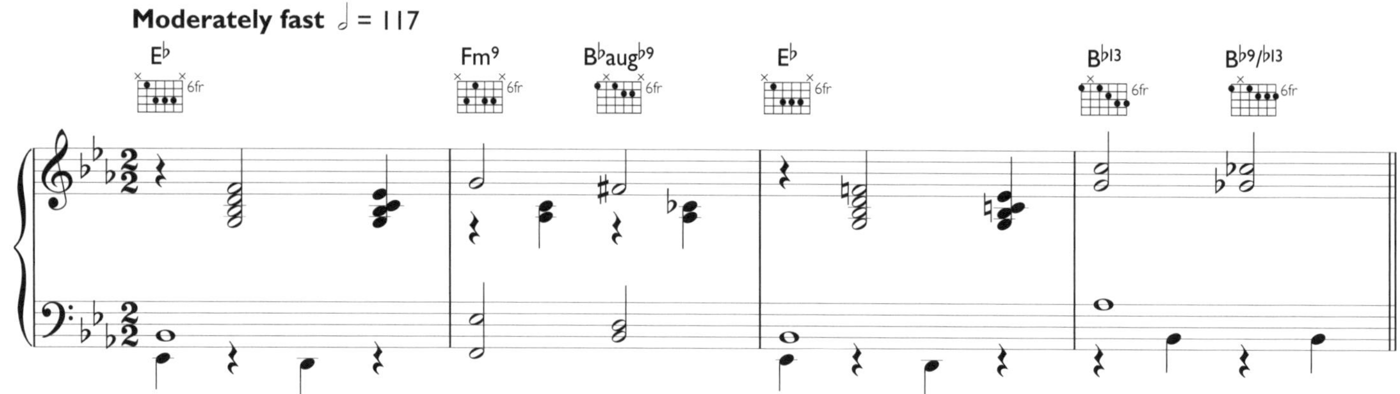

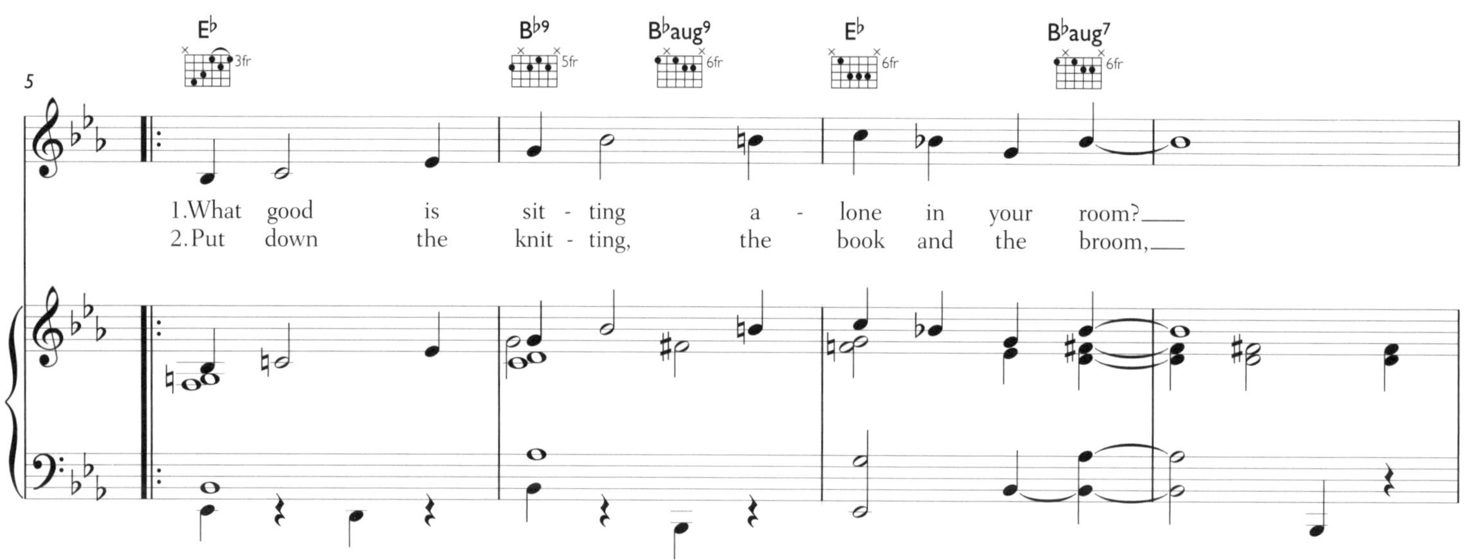

A♭
Adim7
E♭maj7/B♭
C9
Life is a Ca - ba - ret, old chum,
Fm9
B♭9
E♭
Fm7
B♭13
1.
come to the Ca - ba - ret.
2.
E♭
N.C.
A♭m6
- ret. Come taste the wine, come hear the
E♭
Cm
Cm(maj7)
Cm7
F9
band, come blow the horn, start cel - e - brat - ing,
13
17
21
25

Bb7
N.C.
Eb
Bb9
Bbaug9
right this way, your ta - ble's wait - ing,
No use per - mit - ting some
Start by ad - mit - ting some from
Eb
Bbaug7
Eb
Ebmaj7
pro - phet of doom to wipe ev - 'ry smile a -
cra - dle to tomb, is - n't that long a
Bbm7
Eb7
Ab
Adim7
To Coda
way.
stay.
Life is a Ca - ba -
Ebmaj7/Bb
C9
Fm7
Bbll
Eb
ret, old chum, come to the Ca - ba - ret.

29
Coda
D.S. al Coda
N.C.
Come taste the
E♭maj7/B♭
C9
- ret, old chum,
A♭
Adim7
on - ly a Ca - ba -
E♭maj7/B♭
C9
Fm7
-ret old chum, so come to the
B♭♭II
B♭9/♭II
E♭
B♭aug9
E♭
Ca - ba - ret.

CRAZY FOR YOU

Words and Music by John Bettis and Jon Lind

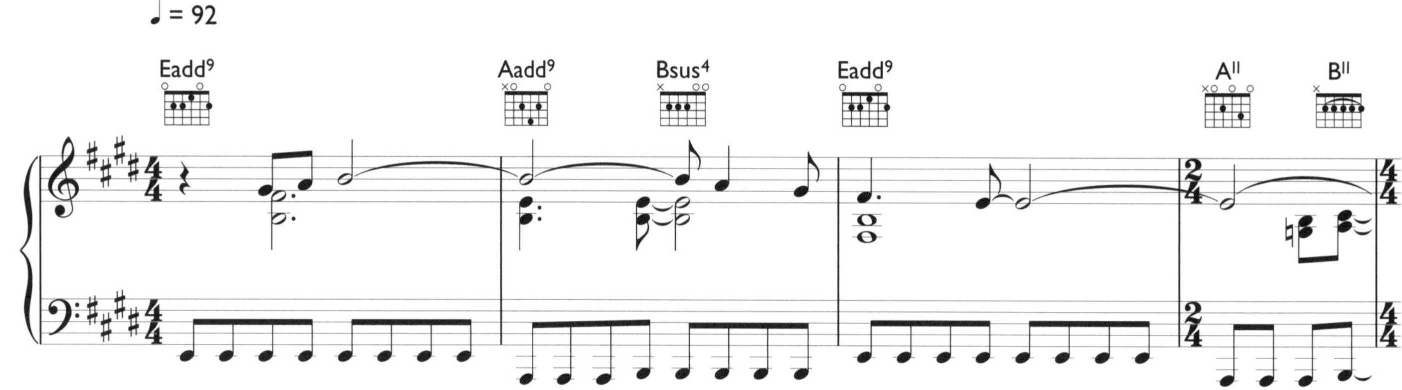

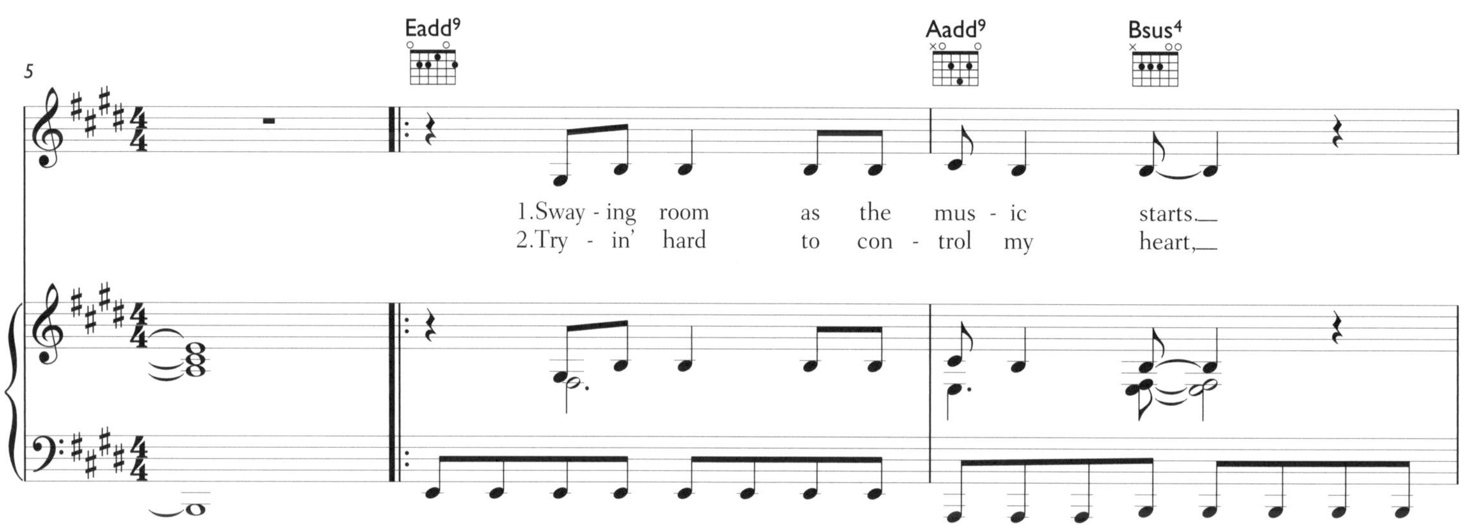

Aadd9 Bsus4 Eadd9 A11 B11
-ies be - come one.
no words at all.
Eadd9 Aadd9 Bsus4 Eadd9
I see you through the smo-ky air.
Slow-ly now we be-gin to move.
Can't you feel the weight
Ev-'ry breath I'm deep-
Aadd9 Bsus4 Eadd9 Aadd9 G#7/B#
of my stare?
-er in-to you.
You're so close but still a world a-way.
Soon we two are stand-in' still in time.
C#m A11 B11 Eadd9
What I'm dy-in' to say; is that I'm
If you read my mind, you'll see I'm
cra-zy for you.

Eadd9/G#
C#m7
Touch__ me once__ and you'll know it's true.__
Ell
Amaj9
Eadd9/G#
I ne-ver want-ed a-ny-one like this.__ It's all brand_ new.__ You'll
1.
F#m7
Bll
E
feel it in my kiss__ I'm cra-zy for you,__
Aadd9
Bsus4
Eadd9
All
Bll
cra-zy for__ you,__

2.
F#m7   C#m7   Am/C   E/B
feel it in my kiss,___ you'll feel it in my kiss be-cause I'm cra - zy for___ you.______
A6   G#7   C#m7   E11
Touch___ me once___ and you'll know it's true.___ I ne - ver want-ed a - ny-
Amaj9   Eadd9/G#   F#m7
-one like this.___ It's all brand_ new.___ You'll feel it in my kiss.___
B11   Eadd9   Aadd9   Bsus4
I'm cra - zy for you,___ cra-zy for___

Eadd9   Aadd9   Bsus4   Eadd9
___ you,___   cra - zy for you,___
Aadd9   Bsus4   Eadd9   A11   B11
cra - zy   for   you.
Eadd9   Aadd9   Bsus4
It's   all   brand   new.___   I'm   cra - zy   for   you.___
Eadd9   Aadd9   Bsus4
Repeat ad lib. to fade
___   And   you   know   it's   true.___   I'm   cra - zy,   cra - zy   for   you.

THE FIRST TIME EVER I SAW YOUR FACE

Words and Music by Ewan MacColl

F
Gsus⁴
And the moon______ and the stars__________
like the trem - - bling__ heart________
And I knew______ our joy________
Em/G
G⁷
C
B♭
were the gifts you gave______ to______ the dark__________
of a cap - tive bird______ that__ was there__________
would fill the earth______ and______ last__________
C
B♭
and the end-less skies,____________ my love.__
at my com - mand,____________ my love.__
'til the end of time,____________ my love__
To____________ the dark__________
That__ was there__________
And it would last__ 'til the end__________
To Coda
1.
C
and the end of the skies.
at___ my com -
'til the end of___

2.
C
30
D.% al Coda
Coda
C
mand,
my love.
time,
my love.
Dm
33
The first time
ev - er I
C/G
G
C
36
saw
your face,
Bb
C
rit.
Bb
C
39
your face,
your face,
your face.

CRY ME A RIVER

Words and Music by Arthur Hamilton

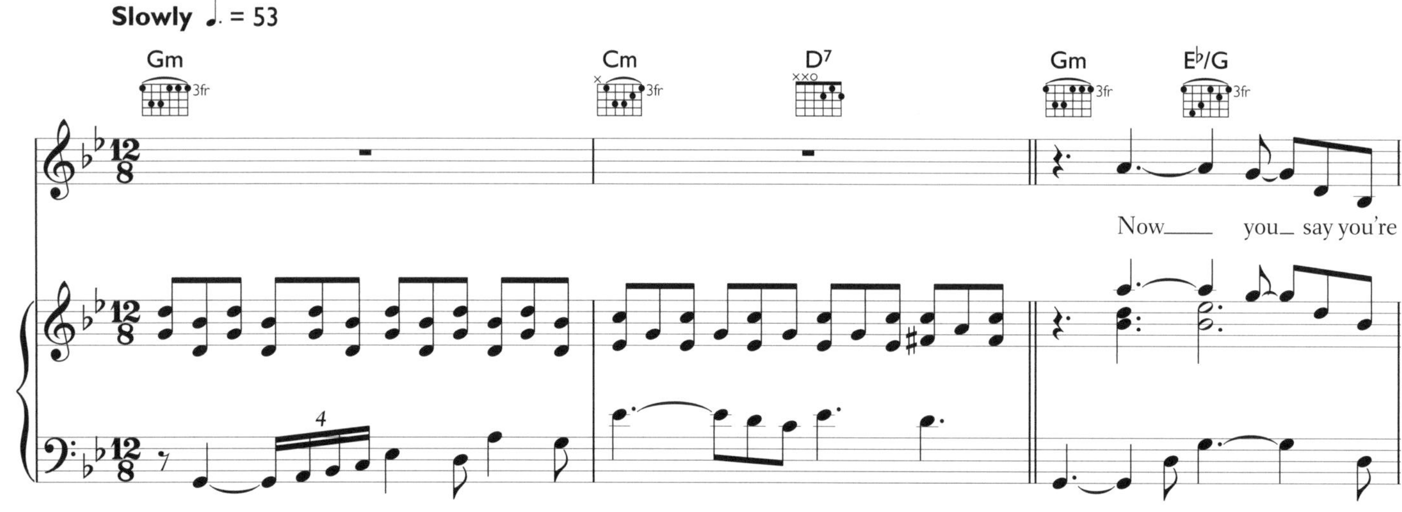

you.
Now you say you're sor - ry
for be - in' so un - true,
well, you can cry me a ri - ver,
cry me a ri - ver, I cried a ri - ver o - ver you.
You drove me, near - ly drove me out of my head, while you nev - er shed a

Gm
A7#9
A7b9
Dm
Gm6
A7#9
tear.
Re- mem - ber,__ I re-mem-ber all that you said,__
Dm
Gm6
D
told me love was too ple - bi - an,
told me you were through with me, an'
Gm
Eb/G
Gm6
Gm7
Cm7
F7sus4
F9
now________ you__ say you love me.________
Well,__ just to prove you
Bb
AmII
D
Gsus4
G
C9
do,
come on and cry____ me a ri - ver,____
cry me a ri - ver,________

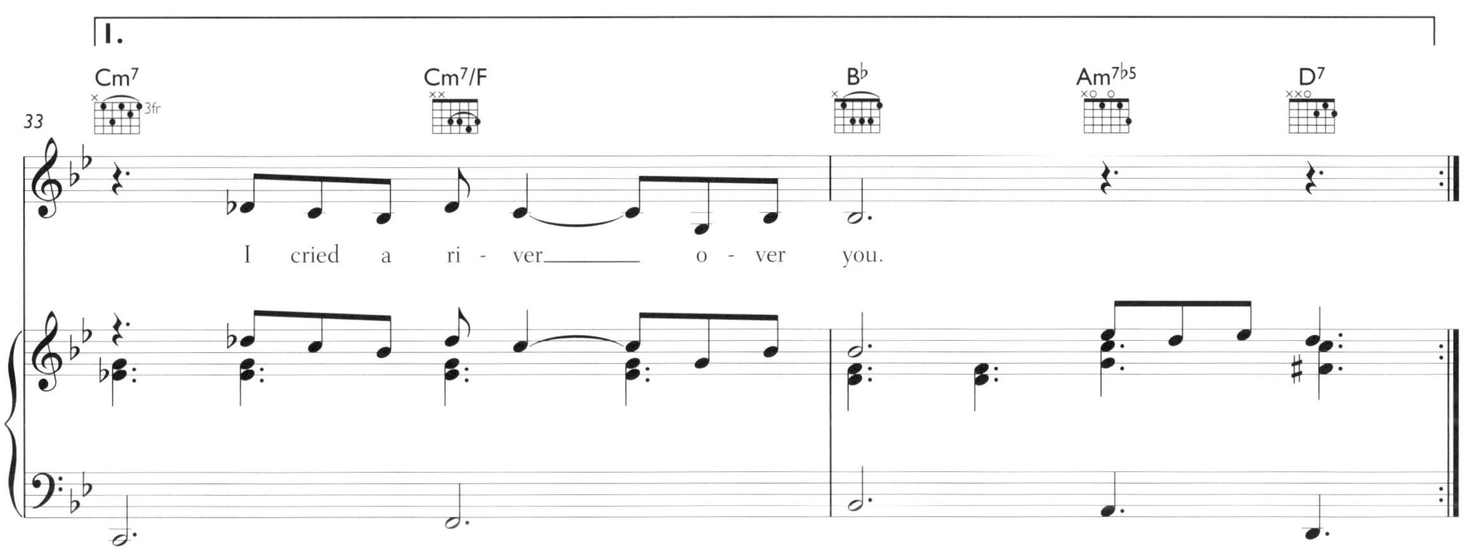
1.
Cm7   Cm7/F   B♭   Am7♭5   D7
I cried a ri - ver____ o - ver you.

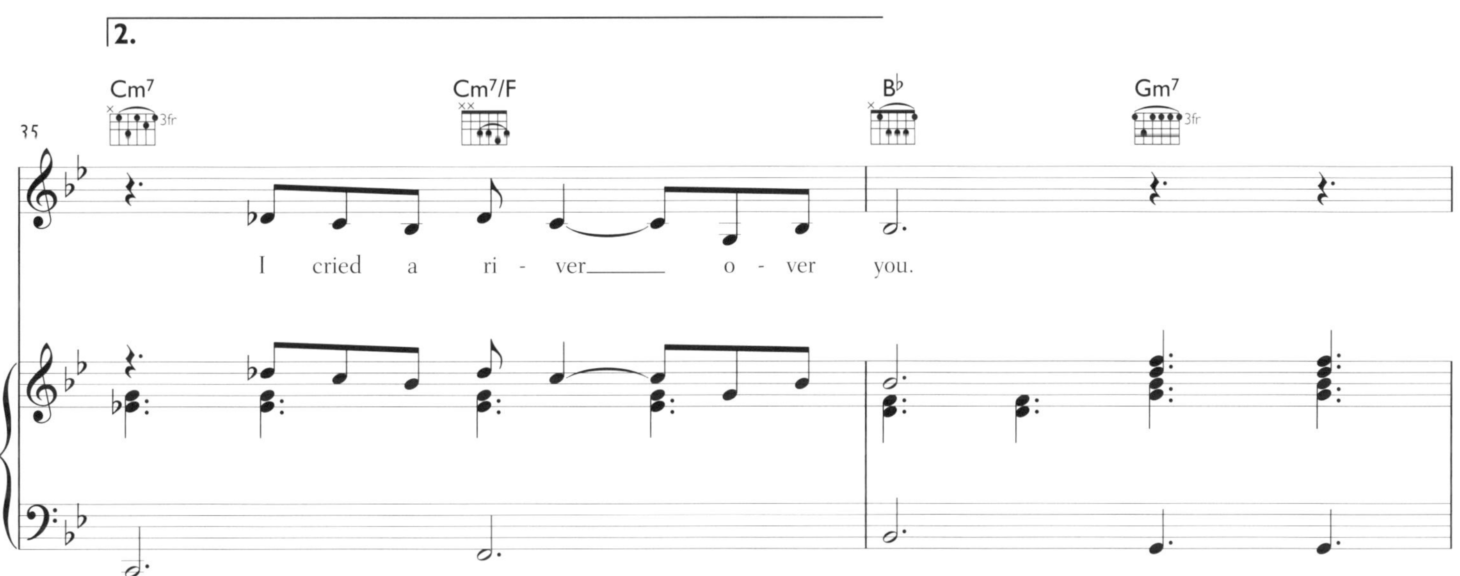
2.
Cm7   Cm7/F   B♭   Gm7
I cried a ri - ver____ o - ver you.

Cm7   Cm7/F   N.C.   slower   Gm
I cried a ri - ver   o - ver you.

DREAM A LITTLE DREAM OF ME

Words by Gus Kahn
Music by Willy Schwandt and Fabian Andre

C
A♭7
G7
C
Say "night - y night" and kiss me, just hold me tight and
A7
Em7♭5
A7
Dm
Dm7
Fm6/D
tell me you miss me. While I'm a - lone and blue as can be,
C
Fm7
G7
C
D9
A♭
A♭6
dream a lit - tle dream of me. Stars fad - ing but
E♭7
A♭
A♭6
E♭7
E♭dim
E♭7
I lin - ger on, dear, still crav - ing your kiss.

I'm long - ing to lin - ger till dawn, dear, just say - ing
this. Sweet dreams 'til sun - beams find you,
sweet dreams that leave all wor - ries be - hind you. But in your dreams what -
- ev - er they be, dream a lit - tle dream of me.

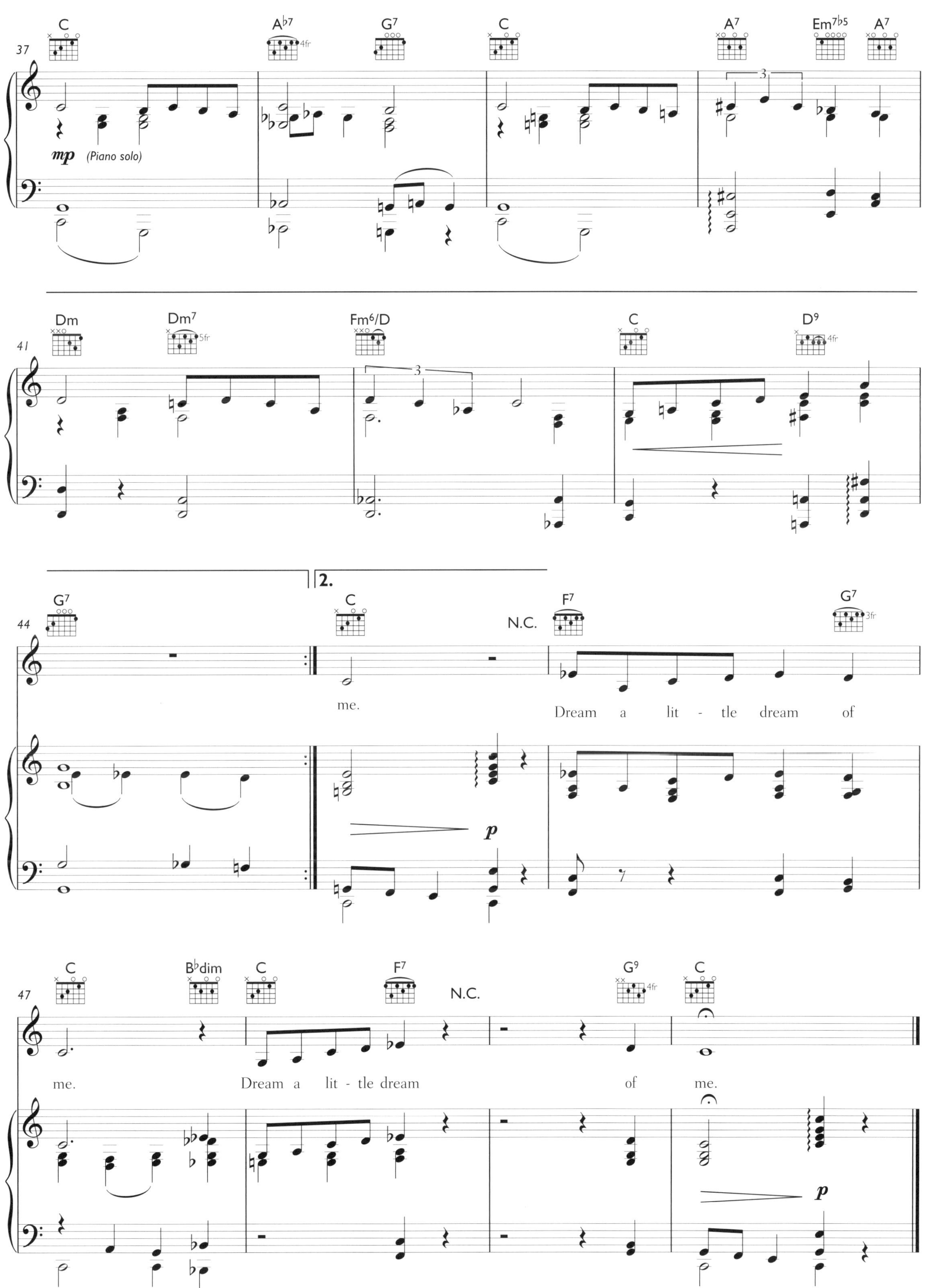

45
C
A♭7
G7
C
A7
Em7♭5
A7
mp (Piano solo)
Dm
Dm7
Fm6/D
C
D9
G7
2.
C
F7
N.C.
G7
me.
Dream a lit - tle dream of
p
C
B♭dim
C
F7
N.C.
G9
C
me.
Dream a lit - tle dream
of
me.
p

FALLIN'

Words and Music by Alicia Augello-Cook

Em   Bm7   Em   Bm7
9
dar - ling___ makes me so con - fused. I_____ keep__ on
Em   Bm7   Em   Bm7
11
fall - in' in and out___ of love with - a you. I_________
Em   Bm7   Em   Bm7
13
nev - er loved some - one___ the way that I love - a you. Oh, oh,
Em   Bm7   Em   Bm7
15
2. I___________ nev - er felt this - a way.___ How do you give me so much

Em
Bm7
Em
Bm7
pleas - - ure and cause me so much pain? Yeah, yeah. Just when I

Em
Bm7
Em
Bm7
think I'm tak-ing more than would a fool, I start

Em
Bm7
Em
Bm7
fall - - in' back in love with you. I keep on

Em
Bm7
Em
Bm7
fall - in' in and out of love with-a you. I

49
25
Em
Bm7
Em
Bm7
nev - er loved some - one____ the way that I love a - you. Oh ba - by,
27
Em
Bm7
Em
Bm7
Em
Bm7
I, I, I, I'm fall - - in'____ I, I, I, I'm
30
Em
Bm7
Em
Bm7
fall - - - in'. Fall,____
32
Em
Bm7
Em
Bm7
fall,____ fall,____

Em   Bm7   Em   Bm7
I____ keep__ on fall - in' in and out____ of
Em   Bm7   Em   Bm7
love with - a you I____ nev - er loved some - one____ the way that
Em   Bm7   Em   Bm7
I love a - you. I'm____ fall - in' in and out____ of
Em   Bm7   Em   Bm7
love with - a you. I____ nev - er loved some - one____ the way that

Em
Bm7
Em
Bm7
I love a-you. I'm_____ fall - in' in and out_____ of
Em
Bm7
Em
Bm7
love with a-you. I_____ nev - er loved some-one_____ the way that
Em
Bm7
N.C.
Em
Bm7
Em
Bm7
I love a-you. What?
Em
Bm7
Em
Bm7
Em

FASCINATING RHYTHM

Music and Lyrics by George Gershwin and Ira Gershwin

D7
Dm
Am/C
E7sus4/B
Am
D9
5fr
out a - ny warn - ing and hangs a - round___ all day.
mf
3
Am
Am7
D/A
Dm/A
E7
I'll have to sneak up to it, some- day, and speak up to it, I hope it lis - tens when I
cresc.
A
Faster
A7
G
A7
G
A7
G
A7
G
say:
"Fas - ci - nat - ing Rhy -thm you've got me on the go! Fas - ci -
p
A7
G
A7
G
A7
D
C
D7
C
-nat - ing Rhy -thm, I'm all a - qui - ver. What a mess you're mak - ing! The

D7 C D7 C D C D7 C D7 G
neigh-bors want to know why I'm al-ways sha-king just like a fliv-ver. Each morn-ing
Em7 F#m Aaug9 D D7 Bm
I get up___ with the sun, (start a-hop-ping nev-er stop-ping) to find at
Bm7 E/B E13 A7 B#dim A7 G A7 G
night, no work_ has been done. I know that once it did-n't mat-ter but
A7 G A7 G A7 G A7 G A7
now you're do-ing wrong; when you start to pat-ter, I'm so un-hap-py.

D7 C D7 C D7 C D7 C D7 C D7 C
Won't you take a day off? De - cide to run a - long some - where far a - way off and make it
D7 G Em6 F#7 Bm Dmaj7/A
snap - py! Oh, how I long to be___ the girl I used to
mf
E7 A7 G A7 G A7 E7 A7
be! Fas - ci - nat - ing Rhy - thm, oh, won't you stop pick - ing on
p
1. D Eb C# B A# 2. D G Bm7 Dmaj7 Em7 Gmaj7 D
me!" me!"
mf cresc. sf

FEVER

Words and Music by Eddie Cooley and John Davenport

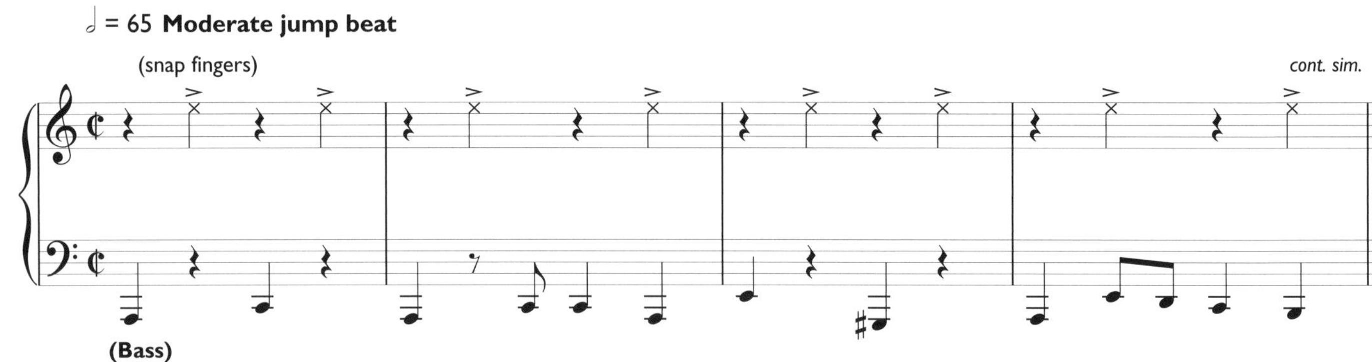

© 1956 Lark Music Ltd, London NW1 8BD

Additional verses

Verse 3:   Romeo loved Juliet,
Juliet she felt the same.
When he put his arms around her, he said,
'Julie, baby you're my flame.'

Refrain: Thou givest fever, when we kisseth
Fever with thy flaming youth.
Fever – I'm afire
Fever, yea I burn forsooth.

Verse 4:   Captain Smith and Pocahontas
Had a very mad affair
When her Daddy tried to kill him, she said,
'Daddy-o don't you dare.'

Refrain: Give me fever, with his kisses,
Fever when he holds me tight.
Fever – I'm his Missus
Oh Daddy won't you treat him right.

Verse 5:   Now you've listened to my story
Here's the point that I have made.
Chicks were born to give you fever
Be it Farenheit or centigrade.

Refrain: They give you fever, when you kiss them
Fever if you live and learn.
Fever – till you sizzle
What a lovely way to burn *(repeat last line to finish)*

FLASHDANCE (WHAT A FEELING)

Words and Music by Giorgio Moroder, Keith Forsey and Irene Cara

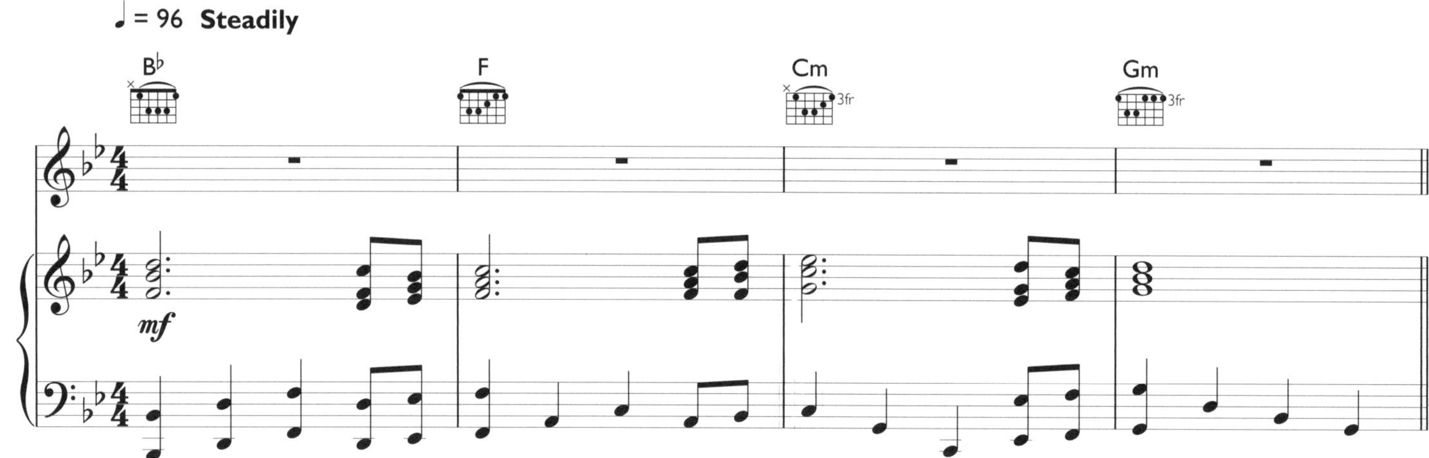

your mind.
All a - lone
I have
cried
si - lent tears
full of pride
in a
world
made of steel,
made of
stone.
Faster, with a driving beat (= 117)
Well,

B♭ F Cm
23
I________ hear the mu - sic, close my eyes, feel the
I________ hear the mu - sic, close my eyes, I am
Gm E♭ B♭
26
rhy - thm. Wrap a - round,________ take a hold of my
rhy - thm. In a flash________ it takes hold of my
A♭ E♭/F F Gm F
29
heart.________
What a feel - ing.
E♭ F Gm F E♭ F
32
Be - in's be - liev - in',________ I can have_

it all now I'm danc - ing for my life
Take your pas - sion and make it hap-
- pen. Pic - tures come a - live, you can dance
now I'm danc -
right through your life
- ing through my life
To Coda

D.% al Coda
Now
Coda
What a feel - ing.

F7
Gm
F
What a feel - ing.
(I am music now.)
Eb
F
Gm
F
Eb
F
Be - in's be - liev - in',
(I am rhy - thm now.)
Pic - tures come
Bb
Cm7
Bb/D
Eb
Fsus4
a - live, you can dance right through your life.
F
Gm
F
Eb
F
Repeat to fade
What a feel - ing.
(I can real - ly have it all.)
What a feel -

GOD BLESS THE CHILD

Words and Music by Billie Holiday and Arthur Herzog Jr.

Bb6 Gm Eb6 Cm7 Bbmaj7 Bb7 Eb6
got his own. Yes, the strong gets more, while the
Bbmaj7 Bb7 Eb6 Fm7 Db7 Bb7/13 Fm7 B7b5 Bb9
weak ones fade, emp - ty pock - ets don't ev - er make the grade;
mf
Ebmaj7 Eb6 Ebm(maj7) Ebm6 Bb/D G7b9
Ma - ma may have, Pa - pa may have, but God bless the child that's
Cm7 F7 Bb6 Eb7 D7
got his own! That's got his own.
p mp

Gm
Gm(maj7)
Gm7
Gm6
Dm
Mon - ey, you got lots o' friends, crowd - in' 'round the
mf
A7
D7
Gm
Gm(maj7)
Gm7
Gm6
door, when you're gone and spend - in' ends,
Dm
G7
F#9
F9
Cm7
Bbmaj7
Bb7
Eb6
they don't come no more. Rich re - la - tions give crust of
p
Bbmaj7
Bb7
Eb6
F7
Db7
Bb7/13
Fm7
B7b5
Bb9
bread, and such, you can help your - self, but don't take too much!

Ebmaj7   Eb6   Ebm(maj7)   Ebm6   Bb/D   G7b9
Ma - ma may have, Pa - pa may have, but God bless the child that's

Cm7   F7   Bb6   Bb9   Bb7/13
1.
got his own! That's got his own.

2.
Bb   A7b5   F7   Bb   A6   Ab13
got his own. He just don't wor-ry 'bout

G7   Cm7   Gb13   F7/13   Bb
no - thing 'cause he's got his own.

THE GREATEST LOVE OF ALL

Words by Linda Creed
Music by Michael Masser

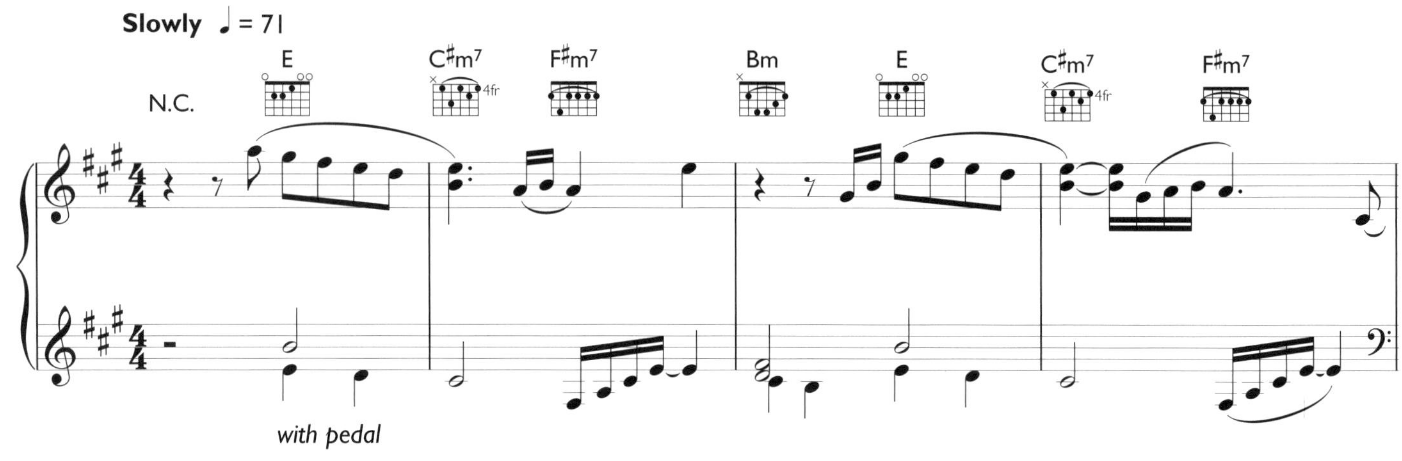

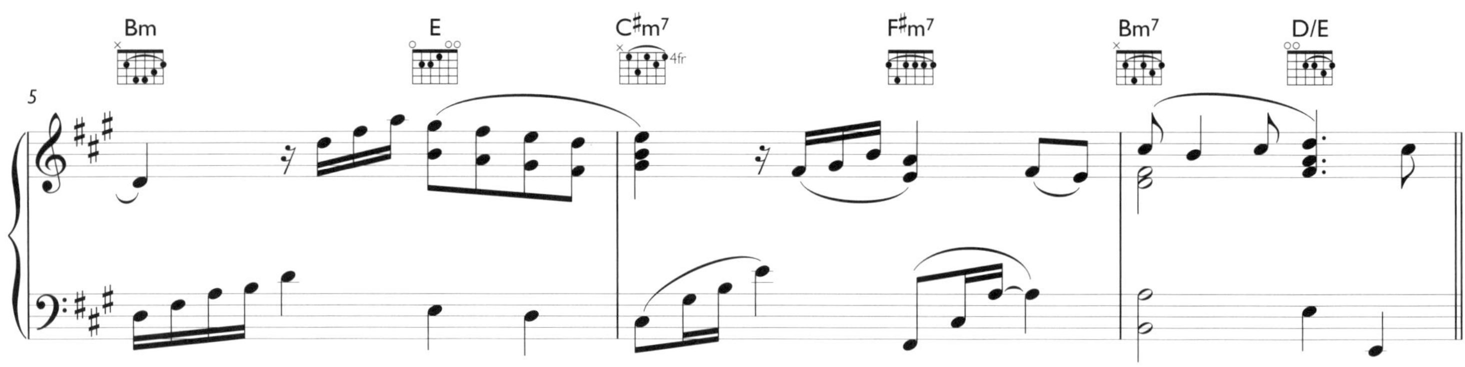

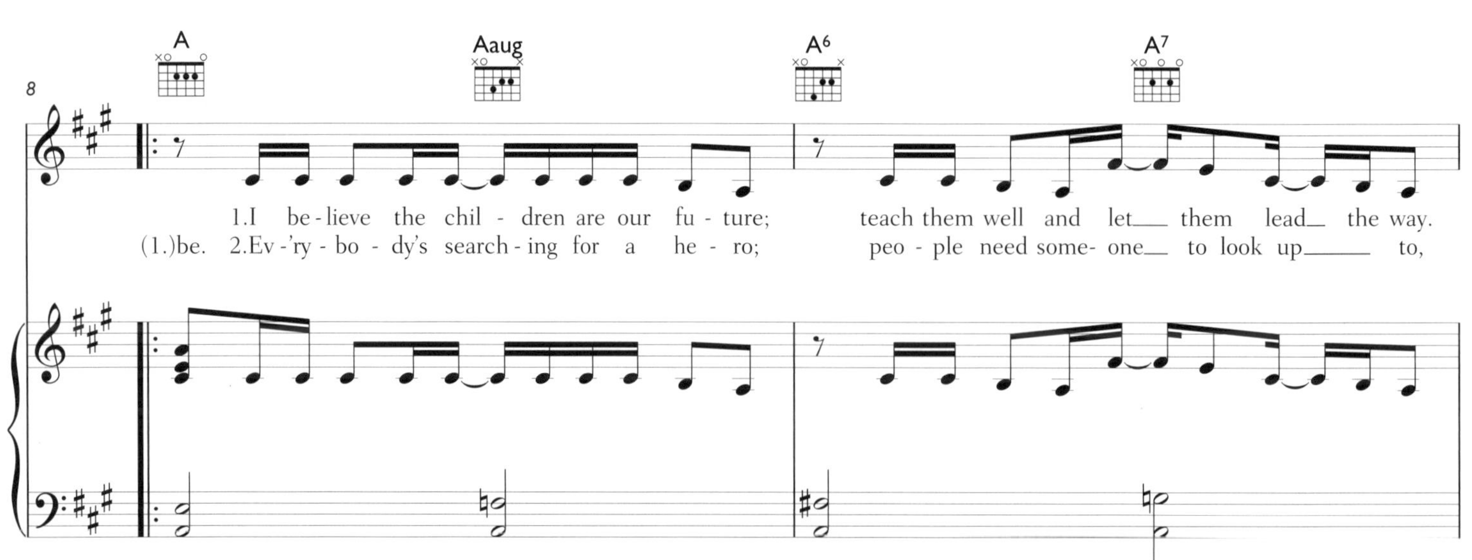

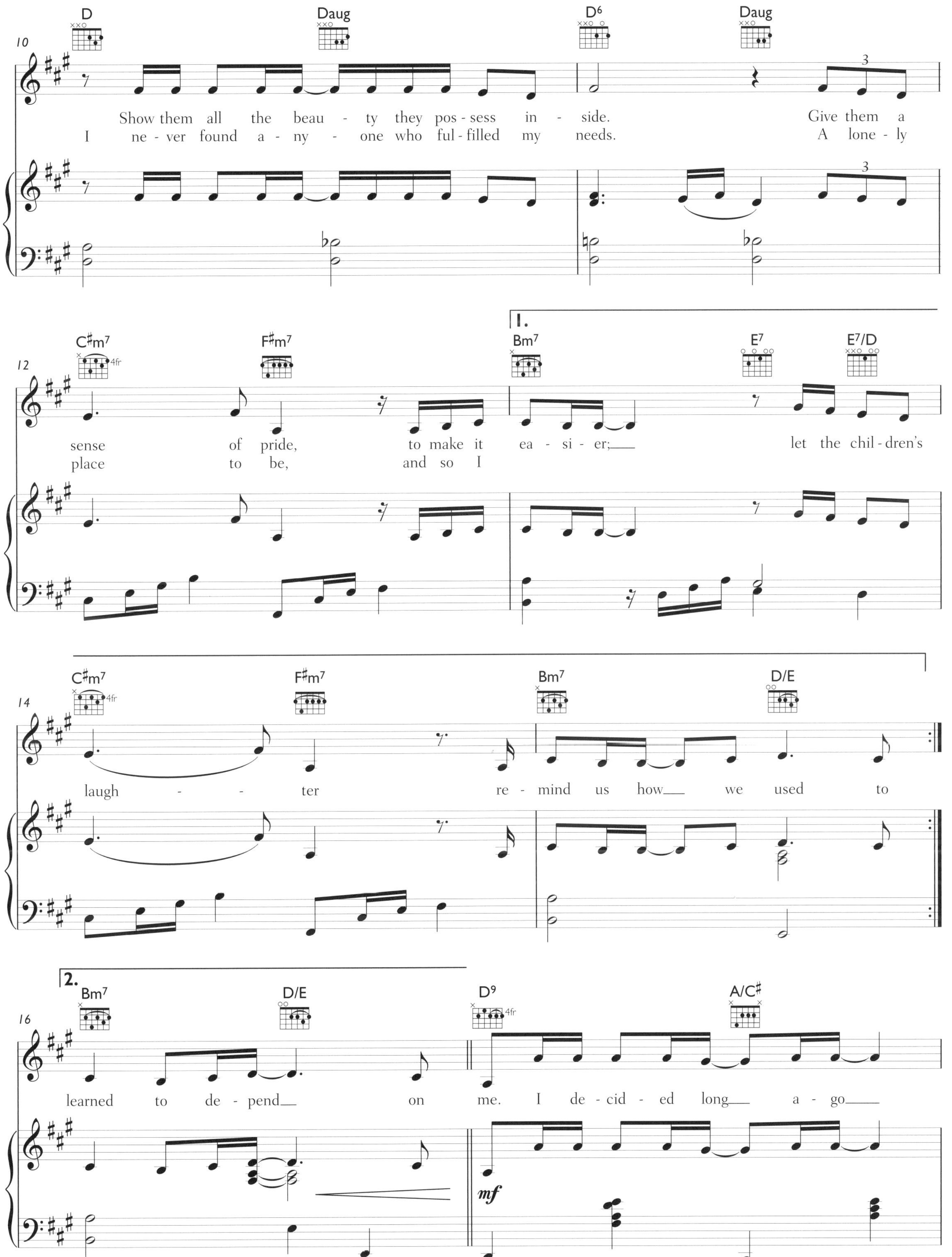
D
Daug
D6
Daug
Show them all the beau - ty they pos - sess in - side.
I ne - ver found a - ny - one who ful - filled my needs.
Give them a
A lone - ly
C#m7
F#m7
1.
Bm7
E7
E7/D
sense of pride,
place to be,
to make it ea - si - er;
and so I
let the chil - dren's
C#m7
F#m7
Bm7
D/E
laugh - ter
re - mind us how we used to
2.
Bm7
D/E
D9
A/C#
learned to de - pend on me. I de - cid - ed long a - go
mf

70
18
Bm7
Bm7/E
D9
A/C#
ne - ver to walk in a - ny-one's sha - dow. If I fail,___ if I suc - ceed,___ at
20
Bm7
Bm7/E
D9
A/C#
least I lived___ as I be - lieve. No mat - ter what they take from me, they
poco rall.
a tempo
22
Bm7
Bm7/E
C#m7
F#m7
can't take a - way my dig - ni - ty. Be - cause the great - - est
25
Bm7
E7
C#m7
F#m7
Bm7
E7
D
love of all___ is hap - pen - ing to me. I found the

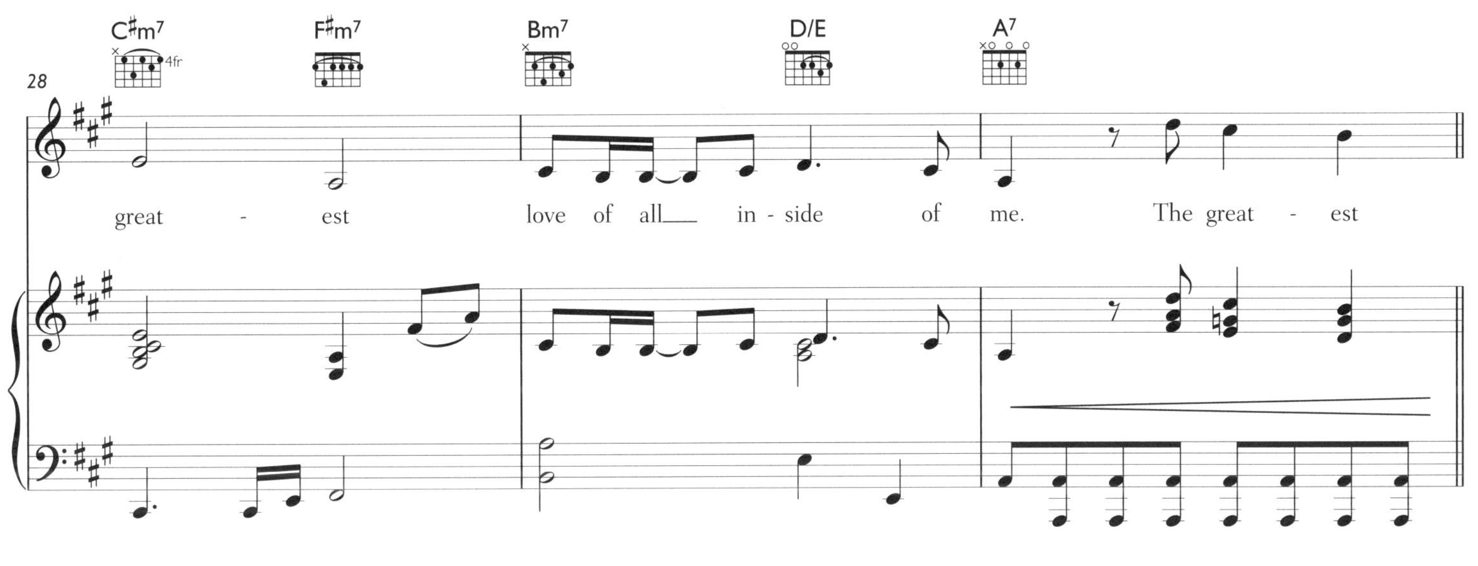
C#m7
F#m7
Bm7
D/E
A7
great - est
love of all___ in - side of me. The great - est

F#m7
Bm7
Em7
A7
A7/G
F#m7
Bm7
love___ of all
is ea - sy to a - chieve.

Em7
A7
A7/G
F#m7
Bm7
Em7
G/A
Learn - ing___ to love your - self,___ it is the great - est love of

72
37
D
E7
E7/D
C#m7
F#m7
Bm7
E7
E7/D
all. And if by chance that spe - cial place that you've been dream - ing
mf
40
C#m7
F#m7
Bm7
E7
E7/D
C#m7
F#m7
of leads you to a lone - ly___ place,
rit e dim.
43
Bm7
D/E
D9
A/C#
Bm7
Bm7/D
Aadd9
find your strength in love.

I AM WHAT I AM

Words and Music by Jerry Herman

F/G   G9   Bbm/G   F   Am
my world, and it's not a place I have to hide in. Life's not___ worth a damn 'til___ you can
Dm   Gm9   C7   F   G
say hey, what I am what I am.   I am___ what I
mf
Bm   Em7   Am11   D   G
am, I___ don't want praise, I___ don't want pi-ty.___   I bang___ my own
Bm   Em   Am   D   G   B/F#
drum, some___ think it's noise, I think it's pret-ty. And so what if I

Em
Aadd9
Cm/A
love each spar - kle and each ban - gle,   why not try to   see things from a   diff -'rent an - gle,
G
Bm
Em
Am
D13
your life___ is a sham 'til___ you can shout   out_____ I   am what   I
Brightly ♩ = 160
G
Ab
am.___   I   am___ what I
Cm
Fm
Bb7
Eb7
am,   and___ what I   am   needs   no   ex - cus - es.________
f

Eb Ab Cm
Fm Bbm Eb Ab
C7 Fm Ab/Bb
rall.
Bb9 Dbm/Bb a tempo A
I deal my own deck, some - times the
ace, some-times the deu - ces. It's one
life and there's no re - turn and no de - pos - it. One
life, so it's time to o - pen up your clo - set. Life's not

C#m
F#m
F#m(#7)
63
worth a damn 'til you can shout
F#m7
F#m6
Bm9
E
67
hey, what I am what
Esus
A
F#m
Bm7
71
I am.
ff
Bbm7/E
A
75

I CLOSE MY EYES AND COUNT TO TEN

Words and Music by Clive Westlake

Ebm/Gb
Ebm
F7
is-n't the things that you say or do, make me want you so.___
Bbm
Ebm
Bbm
It is no- thing to do with the wine, or the
stran-gers a mo-ment a-go, with a
Ebm
Bbm
mu - sic that's flood- ing my mind, and
few dreams, but no-thing to show. The
Ebm/Gb
Ebm
nev-er be - fore have I been so sure you're the
world was a place with a frown on its face, and to -

Cm7b5
F7
slower
some - one   I dreamed I would   find.
mor - row   was just, 'I don't   know'.
It's the
But the
a tempo
Bb
Eb
F7
way   you   make   me   feel,   the mo - ment   I   am close   to
way   you   make   me   feel,   the mo - ment   I   am close   to
Bb
Eb
you,   it's a feel - ing so un - real,   some - how I   can't
you,   makes the day seem so un - real,   some - how I   can't
F7
D7
Gm
be - lieve   it's   true.   The pound - ing   I feel   in   my
be - lieve   it's   true.   To - mor - row, will you   still be

D   Eb   Bb
31
heart,   the hop - ing   that we'll   nev - er   part,   I
here?   To - mor - row   will come,   but I   fear   that
Cb   Gb   Ab
34
can't   be - lieve   this is   real -   ly happen - ing   to
what   is happen -   ing to   me   is on - ly   a
Bb   Bbm
36
me.
dream.   I close my
Bbm7/Ab   Gb   Ebm   F
39
eyes   and count to   ten,   and when I   o - pen them   you're   still

here. I close my eyes, and count a - gain, I can't be - lieve
it, but you're still here. 2. We were
it, but you're still
here, I close my eyes and count to ten, and when I o-
pen them you're still here.
Fade out

I COULD HAVE DANCED ALL NIGHT

Words and Music by Alan Jay Lerner and Frederick Loewe

C9/G   Ab9   FII   F6   FII   F6   FII   F7
could-n't sleep to-night,   not   for   all   the   jew- els
poco cresc.
FII   F7   Bbsus2
N.C.
in   the   crown.   I could have
mf   dim.
mp
Bb   Bbmaj7
danced   all   night,   I could have danced
Bb6   Bb
all   night,   and   still   have

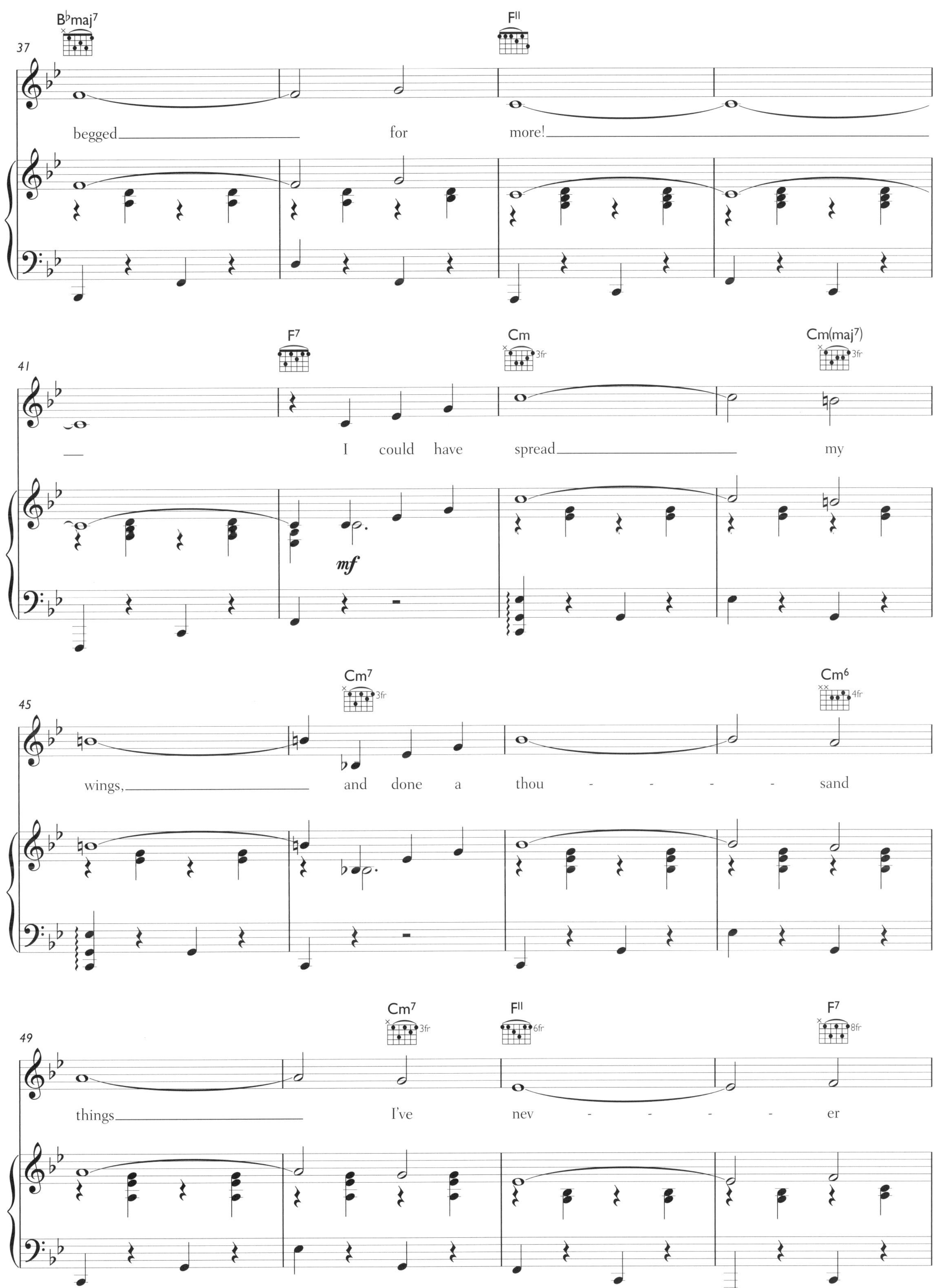

B♭maj⁷
F¹¹
37
begged for more!
F⁷
Cm
Cm(maj⁷)
41
I could have spread my
mf
Cm⁷
Cm⁶
45
wings, and done a thou - - - sand
Cm⁷
F¹¹
F⁷
49
things I've nev - - - er

done be - fore.
I'll nev - er know what made it
so ex - cit - ing,
why all at once my

C11   C7b9   F9   rit.   Eb/Bb
heart   took   flight.________   I
a tempo
Bb/A   Cm7/G   Bb   Cmaj9
on - ly   know________   when   he________   be - gan   to
f
mf
Eb6   Cm7   Ebmaj7/F
dance________   with   me,________   I   could   have   danced,
f
rit.
Cm/F   F11   To Coda 2   F7   To Coda 1
danced,   danced________   all
L.H.
mp

C
N.C.
night!
p
poco a poco cresc.
mp
Meno mosso
F7
mf
f
p
Bb
Bbmaj7
Bb6
(1st maid) It's af - ter three now.
(2nd maid) Don't you a - gree now,
(Both) she ought to
tempo primo
F
N.C.
D.S. al Coda I
be in bed?
(Eliza) I could have
mp

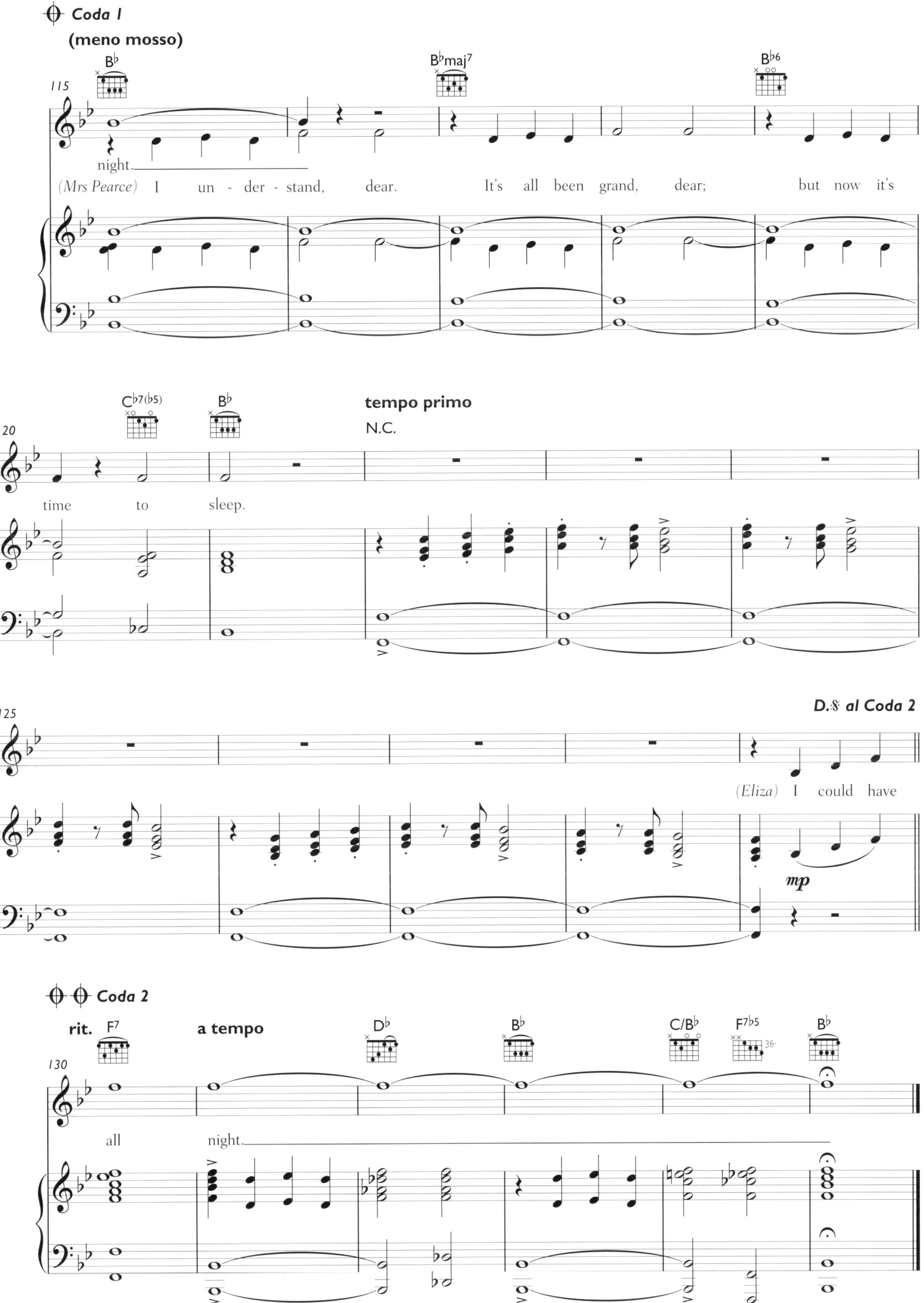
Coda 1
(meno mosso)
B♭
B♭maj7
B♭6
night.
(Mrs Pearce) I un - der - stand, dear. It's all been grand, dear; but now it's
C♭7(♭5)
B♭
tempo primo
N.C.
time to sleep.
D.𝄉 al Coda 2
(Eliza) I could have
Coda 2
rit. F7
a tempo
D♭
B♭
C/B♭
F7♭5
B♭
all night.
mp

KISS ME

Words and Music by Matt Slocum

Fm7   Bb   Eb   Cm   Fm7   Bb
kiss— me—   be - neath the milk - y twi- light,   lead— me—
Ebmaj7   Eb7   Fm7   Bb   Eb   Bb/D
out on the moon - lit   floor,— lift your   o-pen hand   strike up the band   and make— the fire-
To Coda
Cm7   Eb   Abmaj7   Bbsus4   Bb
- flies dance,   sil - ver moon's spark - ling.   So kiss
1.
Eb   Ebmaj7   Eb7   Ebmaj7
me.

92
2.
26
Eb Ebmaj7 Eb7 Ebmaj7
me.
30
Fm7 Bb Eb Cm Fm7 Bb Eb Eb7 D.S. al Coda
3fr
Coda
34
Eb Ebmaj7 Eb7
me.
1. 2.
37
Ebmaj7 Ebmaj7 Eb
So kiss So kiss me.
1. 2.
40
Ebmaj7 Eb Ebmaj7 Ebmaj7 Eb
So kiss

MY BABY JUST CARES FOR ME

Words by Gus Kahn
Music by Walter Donaldson

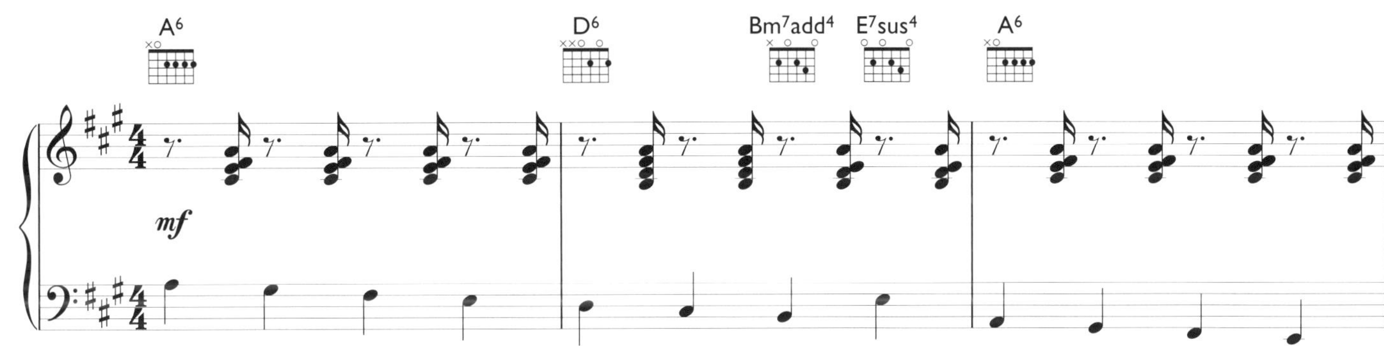

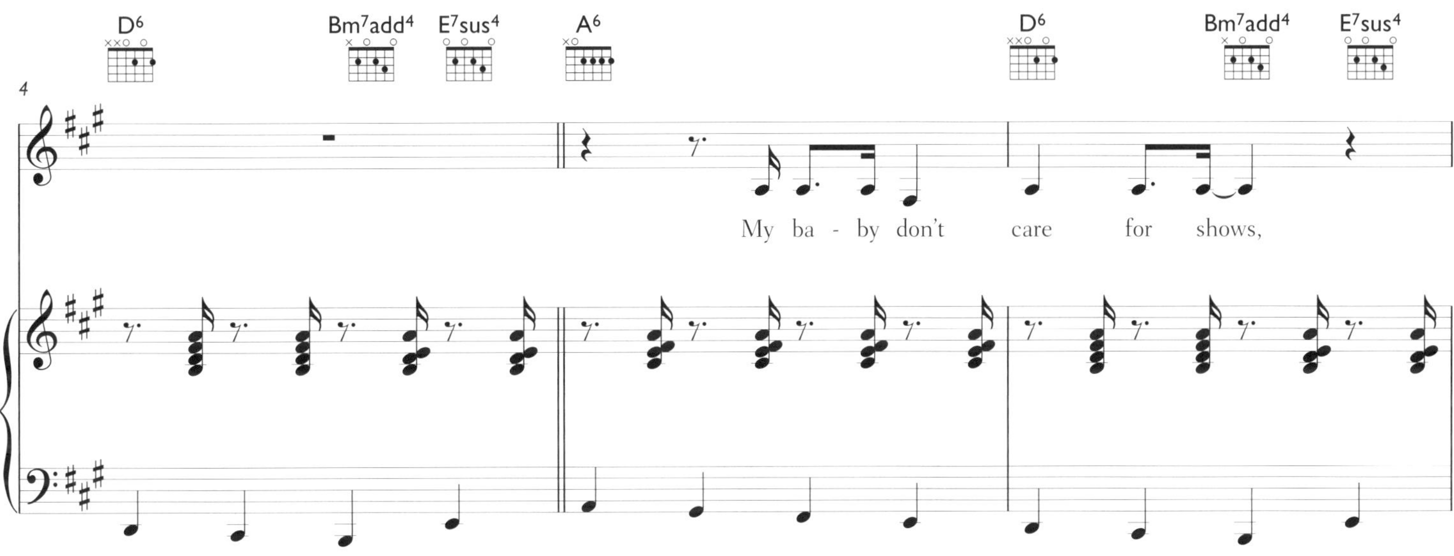

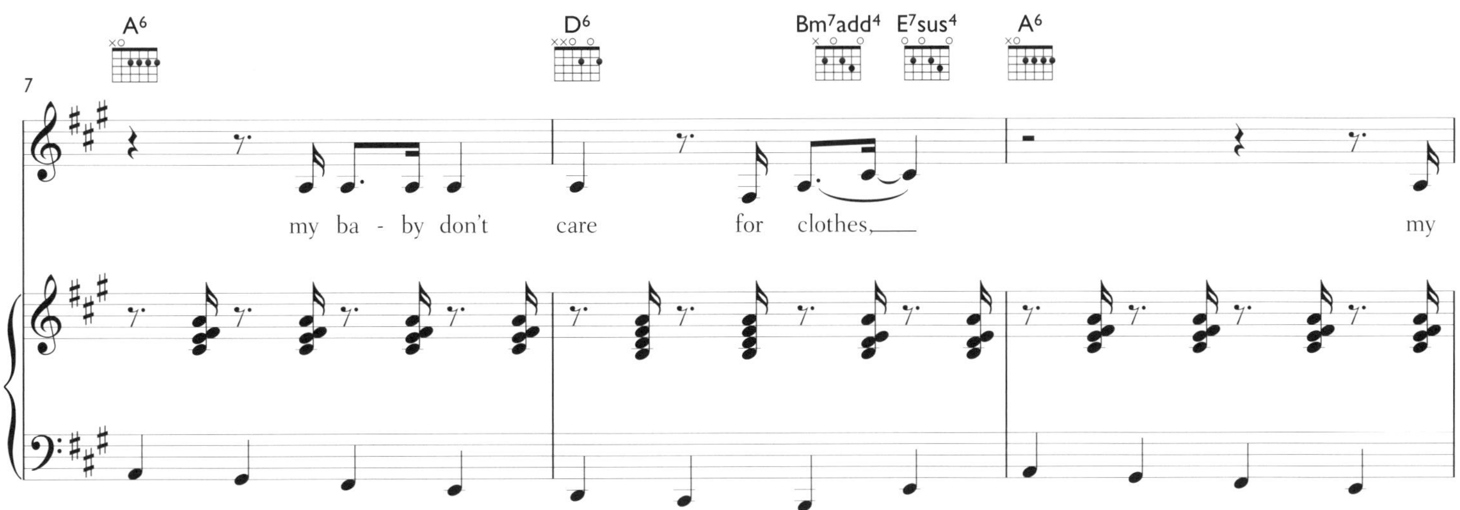

Bm7
E11
ba - by just cares for me.
C#m7/11
C#7
F#m7
My ba - by don't care for cars
B9
and ra - ces, my ba - by don't care for
E11
N.C.
A6
high toned pla - ces. Liz Tay - lor is

D6 Bm7add4 E7sus4 A6 D6 Bm7add4 E7sus4
not his style
and ev - en La - na Tur - ner's smile,
A6 D6
some - thing he can't see.
G#7
My ba - by don't care
A6 A7/G F#7 Bm7
who knows it,
my ba - by just cares

E7
A6
D6
Bm7add4
E7
34
for me.
OPTIONAL SOLO (not included on CD)
To follow CD go straight to bar 69
A6
D6
Bm7add4
E7sus4
A6
37
D6
Bm7add4
E7sus4
A
40
p
Bm7
E11
C#7
43
mp
F#m
46
3
3
3
3
3

B7
E7
N.C.
E7
A6
D6
Bm7add4
E7sus4
subito f
mf
A6
D6
Bm7add4
E7sus4
A
mf
D6

cresc.
ff
Edited audio track re-starts here
mp
Ba- by,   my ba- by don't care for

A6 D6 Bm7add4 E7sus4 A6
71
shows and he don't ev - en care for clothes,
Bm7 E7
74
he cares for me.
C#7 F#m7
77
My ba - by don't care for cars
B9
80
and ra - ces, ba - by don't care for,

E13sus4
N.C.
A6
83
he don't care___ for high toned pla - ces. Liz_______ Tay - lor is_____
mf
D6   Bm7add4   E7sus4   A6
D6
E7
86
not   his   style   and ev - en Li - be - ra - ce's   smiles___
A6
A7/C#
D6
89
3
some - thing_____ he can't____ see.
G#7
4fr
92
Is some-thing he can't   see,_____   I won - der what's   wrong____________

with ba - - - by.
My ba - by just cares
for,
my ba - by just
cares for,
my ba - by just cares
for
me.

MEMORY

Music by Andrew Lloyd Webber
Text by Trevor Nunn after T.S. Eliot

Freely ♩. = 50

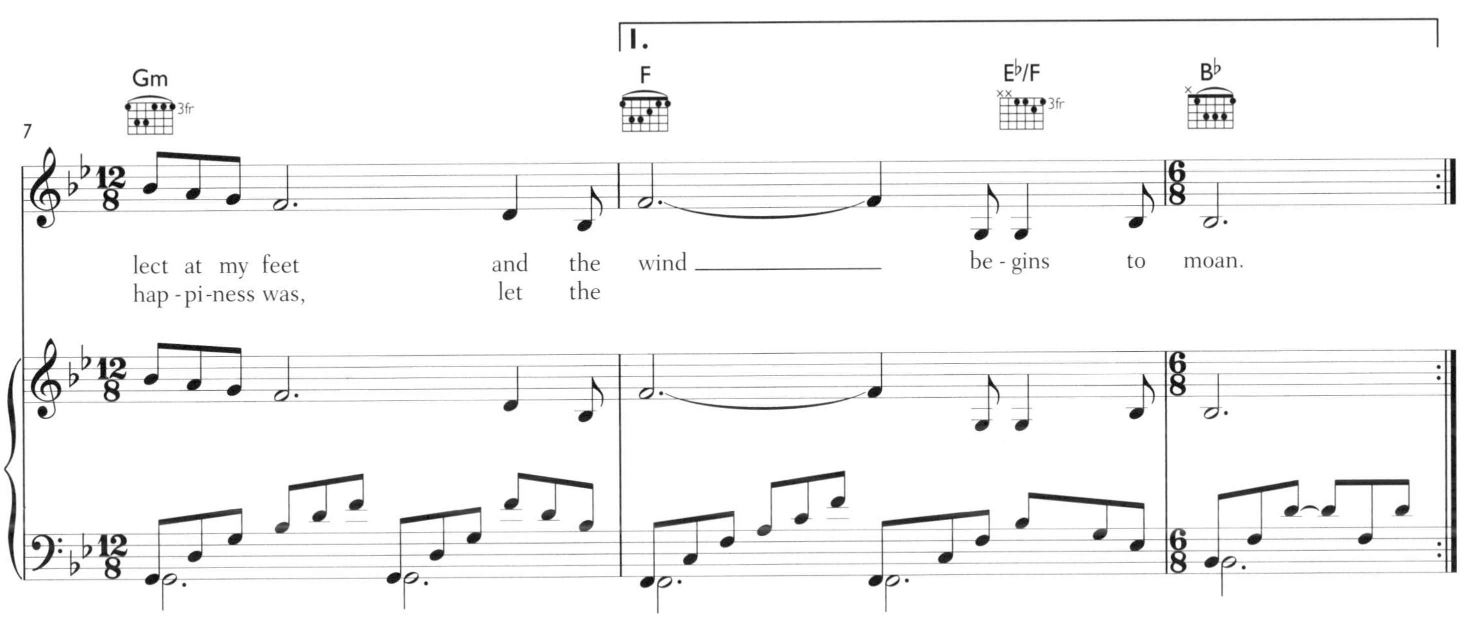

Gm
F
E♭/F
B♭
lect at my feet   and the   wind ___________   be - gins   to   moan.
hap - pi-ness was,   let   the

2. F
E♭/F
B♭
Dm
Dm/E♭ Cm/E♭
mem - ory   live   a - gain.   Ev - 'ry   street   lamp

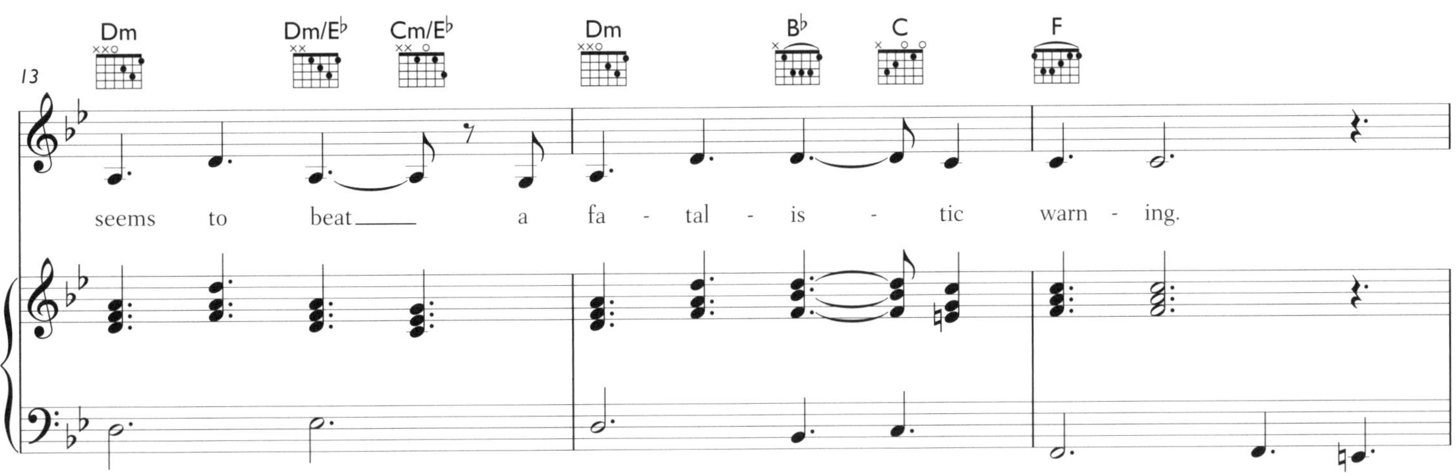

Dm
Dm/E♭ Cm/E♭
Dm
B♭   C
F
seems   to   beat ___   a fa - tal - is - tic   warn - ing.

16
Dm Gm7 C7 Fmaj7
Some - one mut - ters___ and a street lamp gut - ters___ and
18
poco rit.
Dm G7 C
soon it will be morn - ing.
a tempo
20
Bb Gm
Day - light_____ I must wait for the sun - rise,_____ I must think of a
22
Eb Dm
new life_____ and I must-n't give in._____ When the

Cm
Gm
F
E♭/F
dawn comes to-night will be a me-mo-ry too and a new day will be-
B♭
G♭
- gin.
(Instrumental)
E♭m
C♭
G♭
B♭m
B♭m/C♭
B♭m
B♭m/C♭
B♭m
G♭
A♭7
Burnt out ends of smok-y days, the stale cold smell of

D♭
B♭m7
E♭m7
morn - ing.
The street lamp dies, an - oth - er

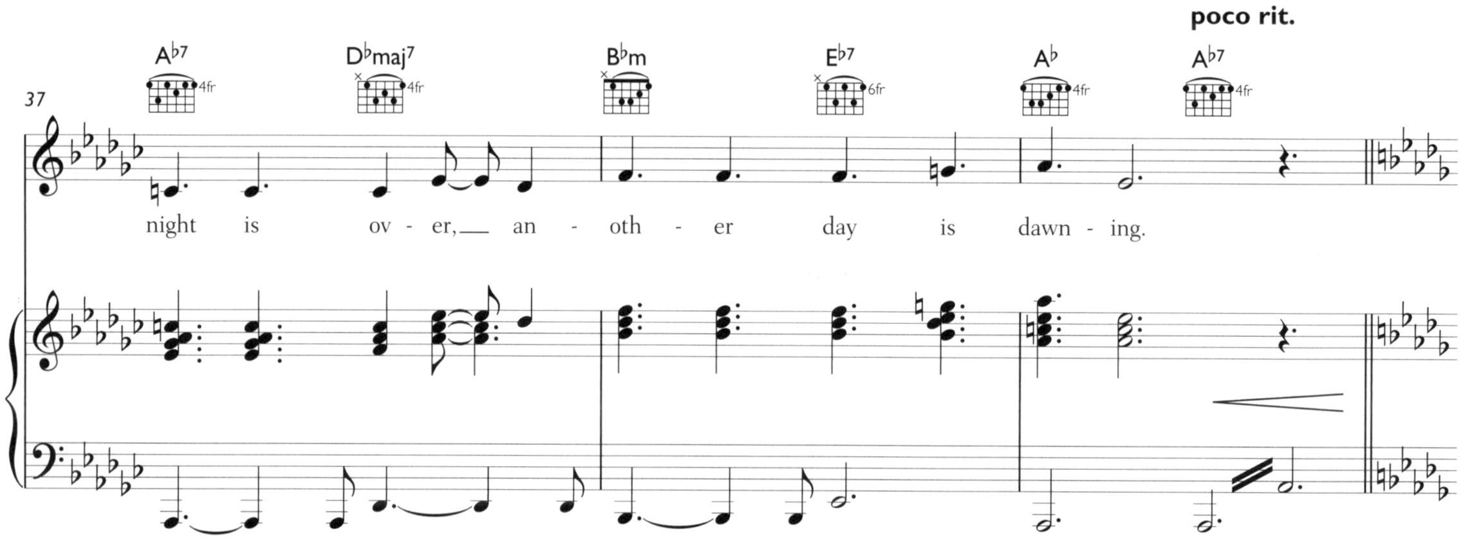
poco rit.
A♭7
D♭maj7
B♭m
E♭7
A♭
A♭7
night is ov - er, an - oth - er day is dawn - ing.

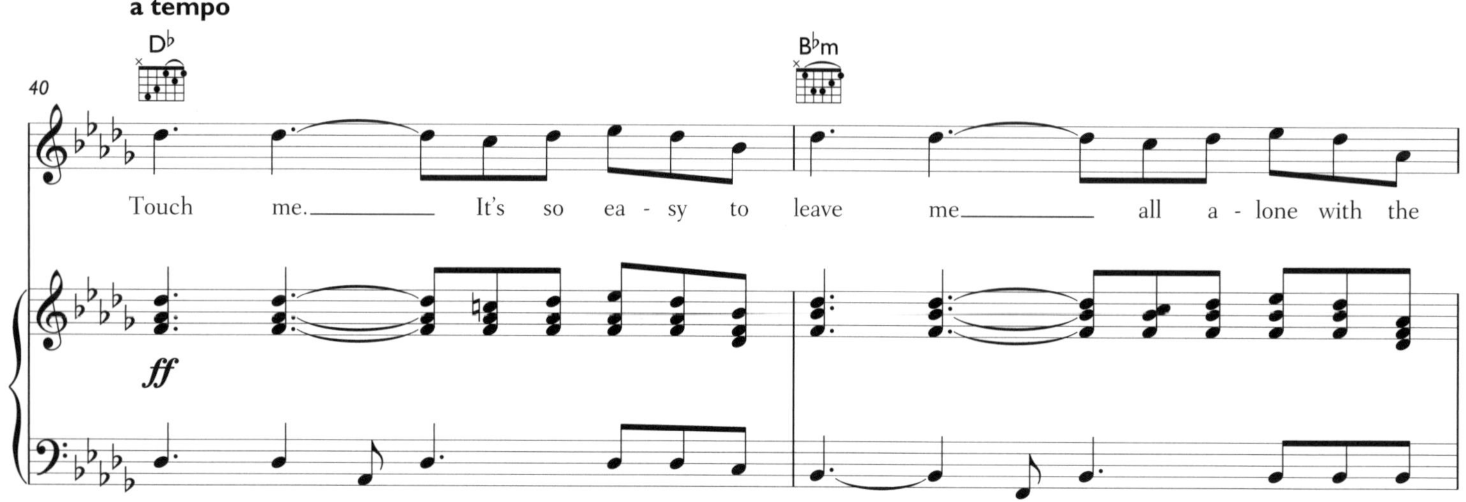
a tempo
D♭
B♭m
Touch me. It's so ea - sy to leave me all a - lone with the
ff

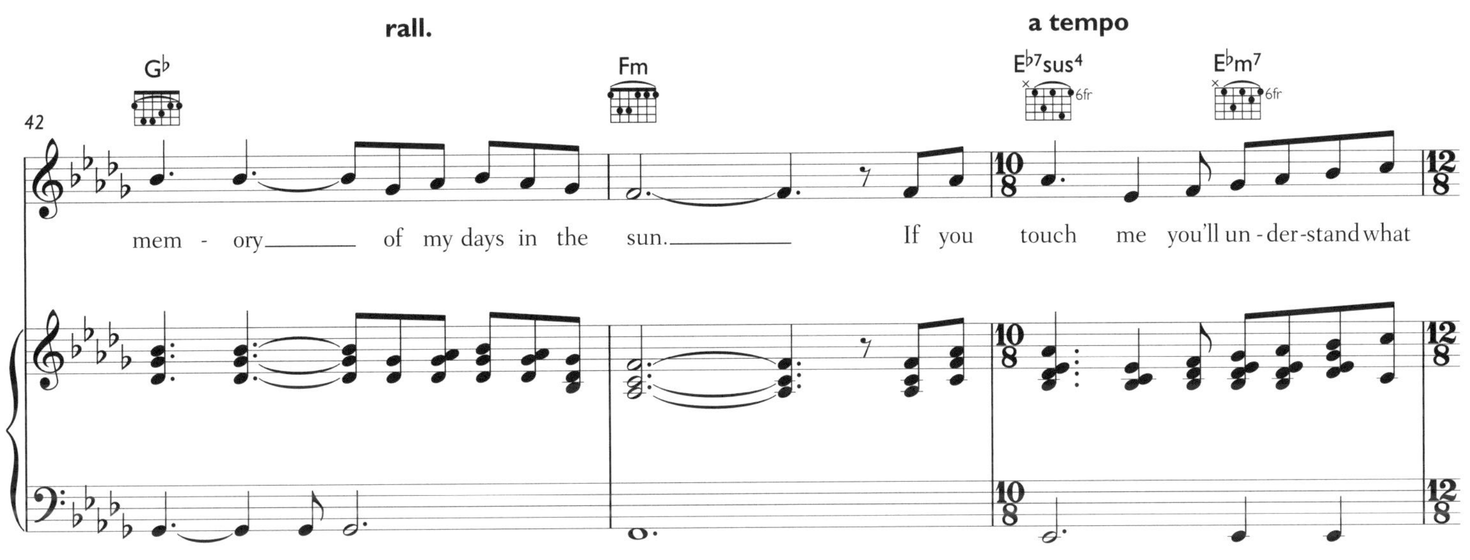

rall.
a tempo
G♭
Fm
E♭7sus4
E♭m7
42
mem - ory______ of my days in the sun.______ If you touch me you'll un - der - stand what

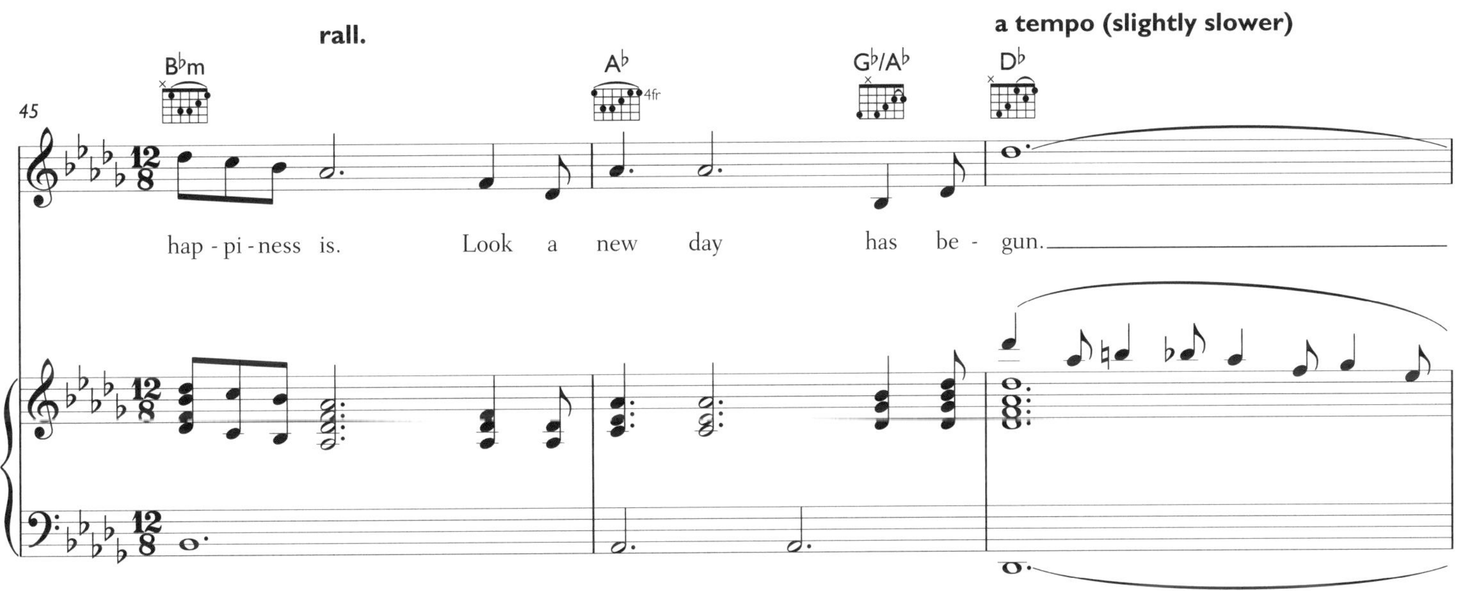

rall.
a tempo (slightly slower)
B♭m
A♭
G♭/A♭
D♭
45
hap - pi - ness is. Look a new day has be - gun.______

48

(YOU MAKE ME FEEL LIKE) A NATURAL WOMAN

Words and Music by Carole King, Gerry Goffin and Jerry Wexler

C/E
Dm7
Em7
Dm7
Before the day I met you, life was so un-
Em7
Dm7
Em7
Fmaj7
- kind. You're the key to my peace of mind, 'cause
Dm7/G
C
F
C
you make me feel, you make me feel,
F
C
F
C/E
C
F
C/E
Dm7
you make me feel like a na - tu - ral wo - man.

To Coda
Dm7/G
C
G/B
2. When my soul was in the lost and found,
Bb
F
you came a - long to claim it.
C/E
Dm7
C
G/B
I did - n't know just what was wrong with me,
Bb
F
'til your kiss helped me name it.

C/E   Dm7   Em7   Dm7
Now I'm no long - er doubt - ful___ of what I'm liv - in'
Em7   Dm7   Em7   Fmaj7   D.S. al Coda
for,   'cause if I make you hap - py I don't need to do___ more___ 'Cause
Coda
C   Bb/C   F
Oh,___ ba - by, what you've done to me!
Backing vocals (What you've done to me!)___
C   Bb/C
You___ make me feel___ so___ good___ in - side.
(Good in - side.)___
3

Fmaj7
Dm7/G
And I just want to be
(want to be)
F
C/E
Dm7
Dm7/G
close to you. You make me feel so a-live! You make me
C
Fmaj7
C/E
Fmaj7
feel, you make me feel, you make me
C F C/E
C F6 C6
Dm7
Dm7/G
repeat to fade
feel like a na-tu-ral wo-man.
You make me
(Wo-man.)

OVER THE RAINBOW

Words by E Y Harburg
Music by Harold Arlen

Db
Dbm7
Ab
Ab/G
in _______ a _____________________ land __
and _______ the _____________________ dreams
Fm
Bbm7
Eb7sus4
Eb7/G
that I __ heard of once, once in a lul -
that you __ dared to dream real - ly do _____________
Abadd9
1.
Bbm7
Eb/G
2.3.
Bbm7
Eb/G
- la - by.
__ come true.
(2.)*Some __
Abadd9
Ab5
Abadd9
Ab5
Abadd9
Ab5
Abadd9
Ab5
Bbm7
Bb7sus4
Bbm7
Bb7sus4
__ day __ I'll __ wish up - on a star and wake up __ where the

E♭7/G
A♭maj9
Fm
clouds   are   far________________ be - hind   me.
B♭m7
B♭m9
Cm/E♭
E♭9/G
A♭add9
A♭5
A♭add9
A♭5
Where______   trou - bles
A♭add9
A♭5
A♭add9
A♭5
G7
melt   like   le - mon drops   a - way a - bove______ the chim - ney tops,   that's
To Coda
D.S. al Coda
Cm
Cm/B
B♭m7
E♭7/G
where__________   you'll__________   find____   me.

Coda
rit.
B♭m7
E♭7/G
me.
a tempo
A♭5
Fm
Cm7
A♭7
Some - where___ ov - er___ the rain - bow___
D♭
D♭m7
A♭add9
A♭7
A♭sus4/B♭
A♭/C
skies___ are blue___ and___
D♭
D♭m7
A♭
A♭5/G
Fm
the___ dreams___ that you dared to___

dream real - ly do come true. If
hap - py lit - tle blue - birds fly a - bove the rain - bow,
why, oh why can't I?
rit.
a tempo
rubato
a tempo
rit.

THE POWER OF LOVE

Words and Music by Candy De Rouge,
Gunther Mende, Jennifer Rush and Mary Applegate

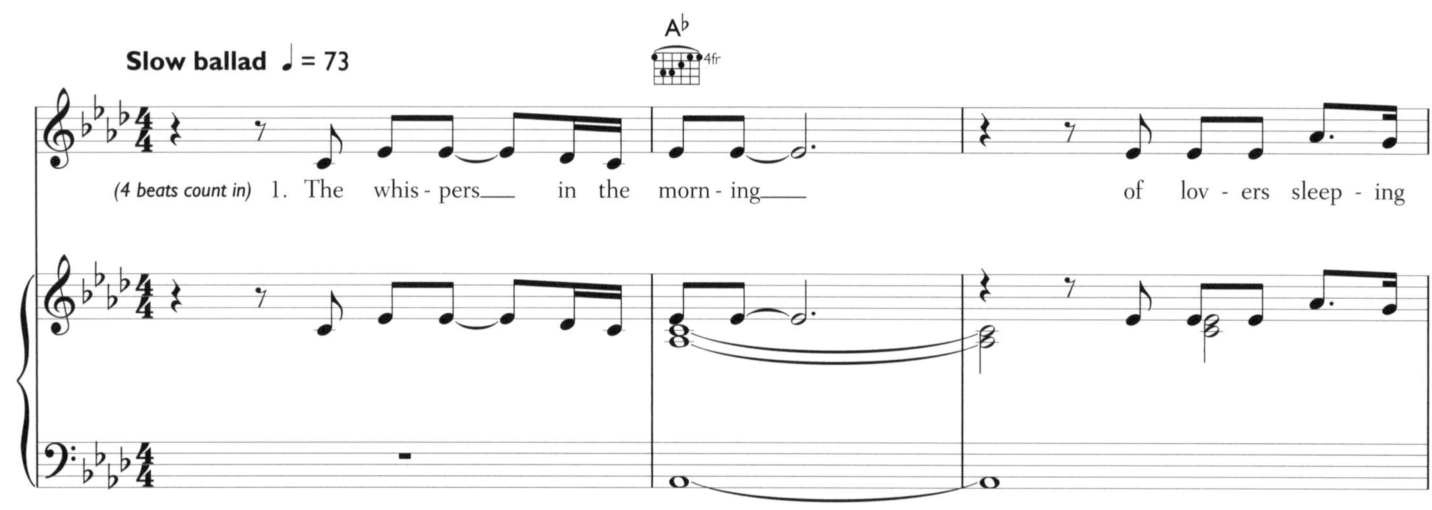

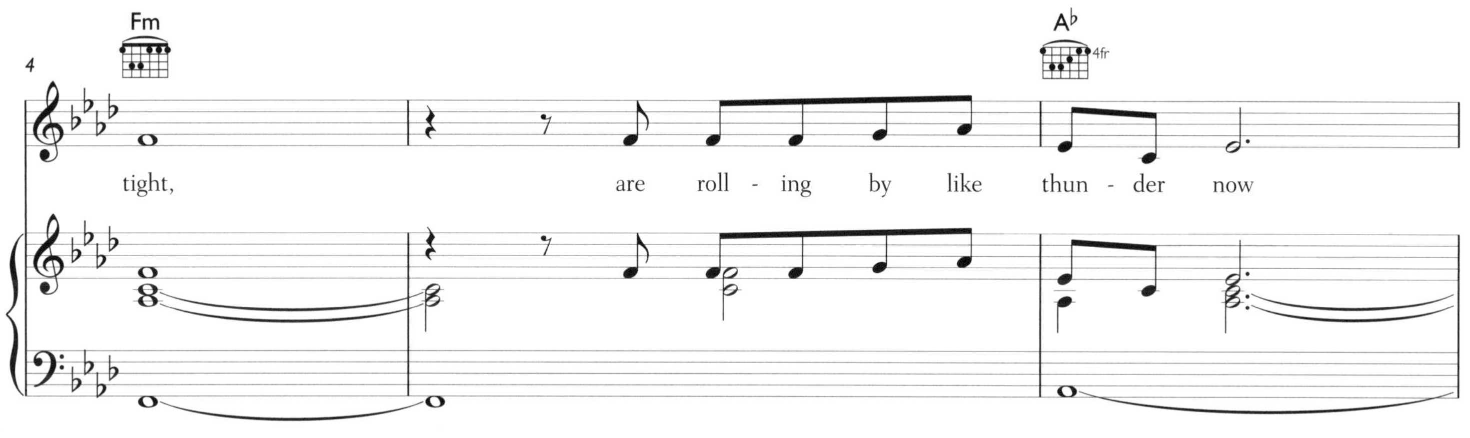

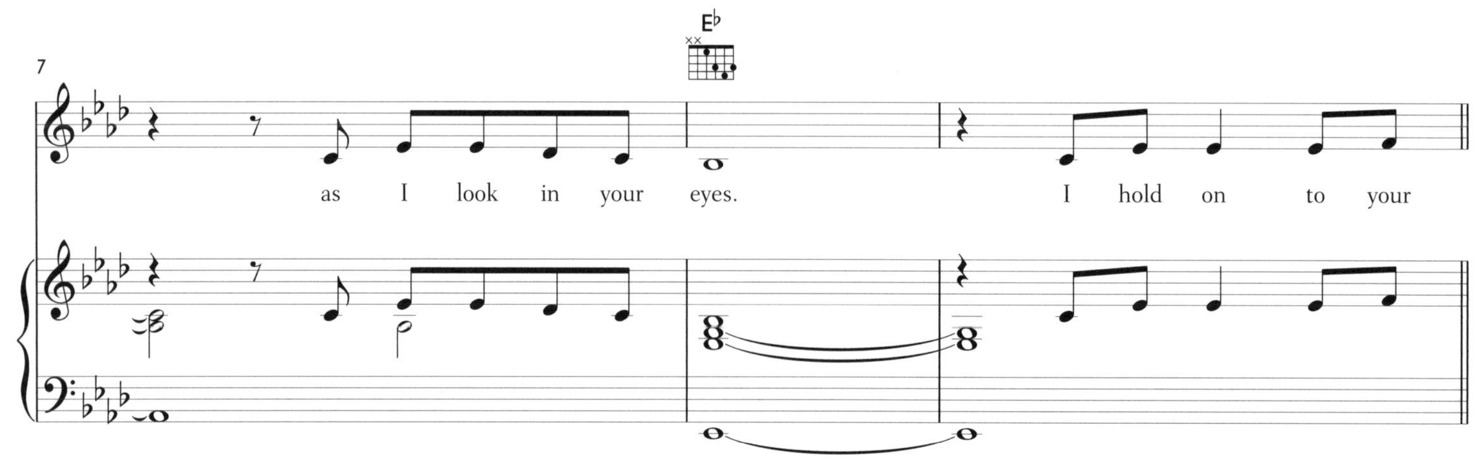

Ab
Fm
bo - dy,___
(2.) times___
and feel each move you make,
it seems I'm far a - way,
Db
Ab/C
your voice is warm and ten - der,
but ne - ver won - der where I am
a love that I could
'cause I am al - ways
not for -
by your
Eb
Ab
- sake.}
side.}
'Cause I am your la - dy,___
Db
and you are my man,___
when - ev - er you reach___

B♭m
E♭
E♭11
for me,
I'll do all that I can.
I'm gon-na do all that I can.
1.
2. 3.
E♭
E♭
A♭ 4fr
2. Ev-en though there may be
We're head-ing for some - thing,
D♭
some-where I've ne - ver been,
some-times I am fright-
B♭m
A♭ 4fr
E♭
D♭
To Coda
A♭ 4fr
- ened, but I'm rea - dy to learn
'bout the pow - er of love.

The sound of your heart beat - ing
made it clear sud - den - ly,
and feel - ing that I
can't go on
is light years a - way.
D.% al Coda
'Cause I am your la -
Coda
Repeat to fade
The pow-er of love.

STORMY WEATHER

Words by Ted Koehler
Music by Harold Arlen

Slow lament, slightly swung ♩ = 66

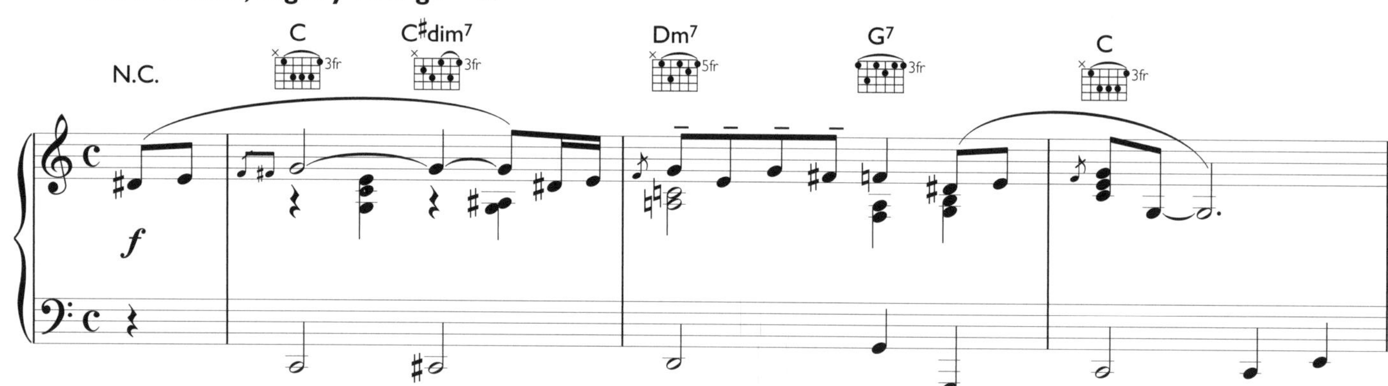

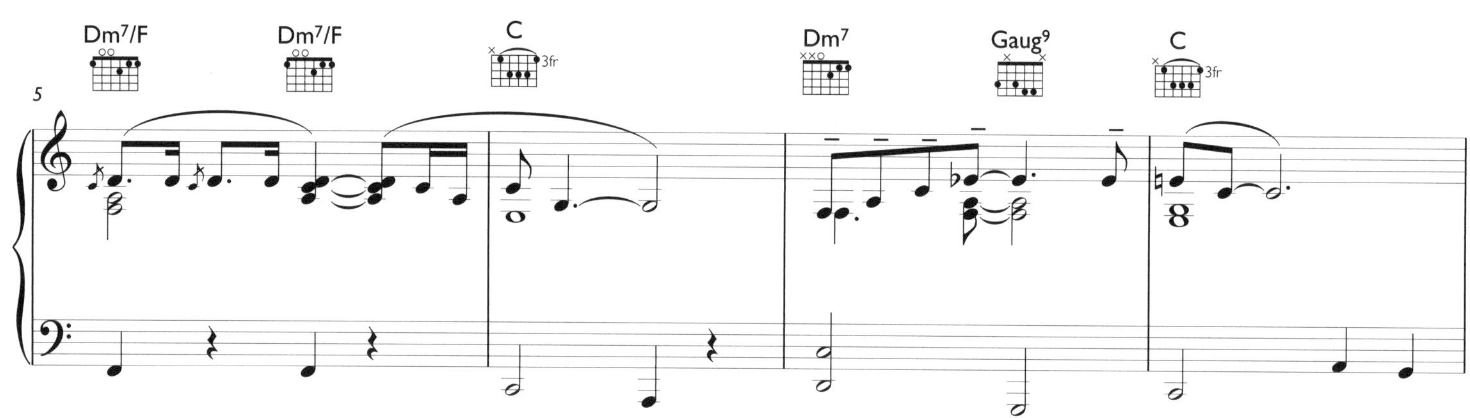

weather. Since my man and I ain't to-geth-er,
keeps rain-in' all the time. My life is
bare, gloom and mis-'ry ev-'ry where, storm-y wea-ther.
Just can't get my poor self to-geth-er, I'm wea-ry all the

C
F C
C#dim7
Dm7
Gaug9
time,___ the time.___ So wea-ry all___ the
C
F
Fm
C
time.___ When he went a-way___ the blues walk'd in and met me,___
F
Fm
C
F C
F
Fm
if he stays a-way___ old rock-in' chair will get me.___ All I do is pray___ the Lord a-
C
F C/G
C
A7b5
D7
G7
-bove will let me___ walk in the sun once more. Can't go

on, ev-'ry-thing I had is gone, storm-y wea-ther.
Since my man and I ain't to-geth-er, keeps rain-in' all the
time. Keeps rain-in' all the time.
Don't know time.
pp

SUNRISE

Words and Music by Norah Jones and Lee Alexander

Cm7   Ab   Eb   Cm7 Bb6 Eb Ab
af - ter - noon's al - rea - dy come_ and gone.   And I said "Ooo,_____
Cm7 Bb6 Eb Ab
ooo,_____
Cm7 Bb6 Eb Ab   Fm9   Bbsus4   Cm7
ooo,"_____   to you.   2. Sur - prise,   sur - prise,   could-n't
Bbsus4   Eb   Cm7   Eb   Ab   Eb
find it in your eyes,   but I'm sure it's writ - ten all o - ver my face.   Sur -

Gm7 Cm7 B♭sus4 E♭ Cm7 A♭
-prise, sur-prise, ne-ver some-thing I could hide,_ when I see we made it through an-oth-er day,_
E♭ Cm7 B♭6 E♭ A♭ Cm7 B♭6 E♭ A♭
then I say "Ooo,_____ ooo,_____
Cm7 B♭6 E♭ A♭ Fm9
ooo",_____ to you._
B♭sus4 Cm7 B♭sus4 E♭ Cm7 E♭ A♭

Now the night,
will throw its cov-er down, mmm on me a-gain,
oo and if I'm right, it's the on-ly way to

bring me back. "Ooo, ooo,
ooo" to you.
"Ooo, ooo,
ooo", to you

TOTAL ECLIPSE OF THE HEART

Words and Music by Jim Steinman

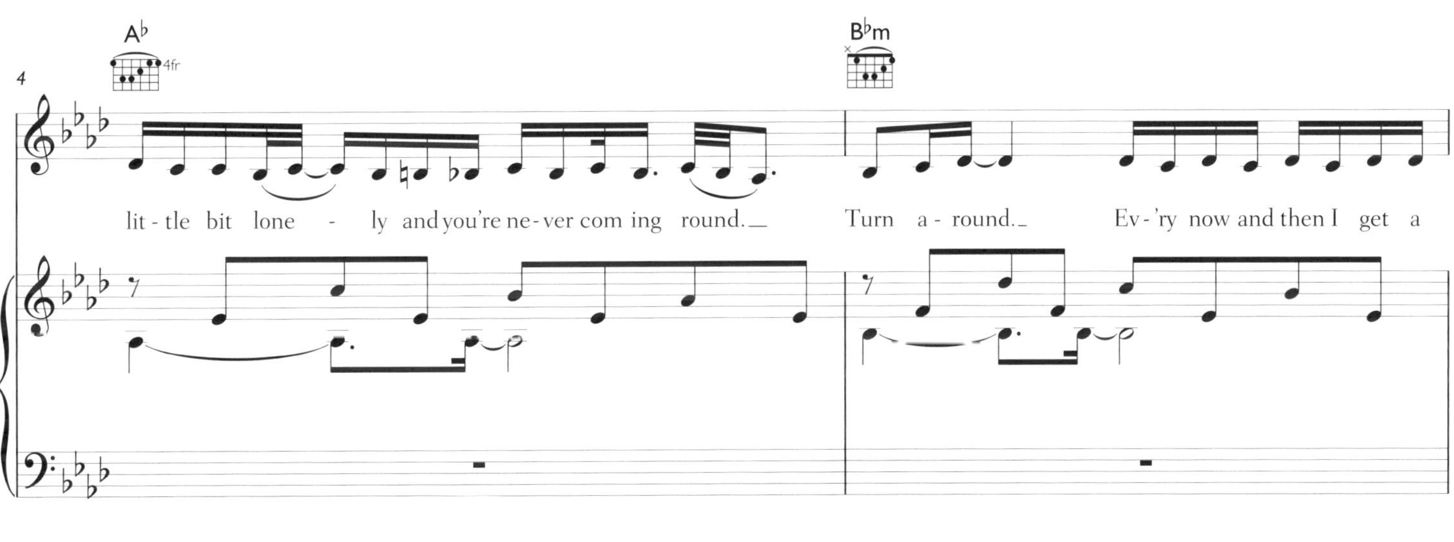

lit - tle bit ner - vous that the best of all the years have gone by. Turn a - round.__ Ev - 'ry now and then I get a
lit - tle bit ter - ri - fied and then I see the look in your eyes. Turn a - round bright_ eyes.
Ev - 'ry now and then I fall a - part. Turn a - round_ bright_ eyes. Ev - 'ry now and then I fall a -
- part and I need you now__ to - night, and I need you more_ than ev -

Ab
Fm
Db
Eb7
- er.   And if you on - ly hold___ me tight,   we'll be hold - ing on________ for -
Ab
Fm
Db
Eb7
- ev - er,   and we'll on - ly be mak - ing it   right_____ 'cause we'll ne - ver be wrong_____ to -
Db/F
Eb/G
Fm
Bb
- geth - er. We can take it to the end of the line,   your love is like a sha-dow on me all of the time.____
Ab
Eb/G
I   don't know what to do and I'm al - ways in the dark,___ we're

Fm
B♭
liv-ing in a pow-der keg and giv-ing off sparks.___ I real-ly need you to-night,
A♭/C
E♭/B♭
A♭/C
D♭
E♭7
for-ev-er's gon-na start to - night,___ for-ev-er's gon-na start__ to -
A♭/E♭
Fm
C
Once up-on a time I was fall-ing in love, but now I'm on-ly fall-ing a-part.
-night.
D♭
A♭/C
B♭m7
E♭
To Coda
There's no-thing I can do, a to-tal e-clipse__ of the heart.

Ab Fm Db Eb7 Eb7/G Ab Fm
33
Once up-on a time there was light in my life, but
C Db Ab/C Bbm7 Eb
36
now there's on - ly love in the dark. No-thing I can say, a to -tal e - clipse_ of the heart.
Ab Fm Db Eb7 Eb7/G Ab
38
D.% al Coda
Coda
Ab Fm Eb7 Db Eb7 Eb7/G
41
Repeat to fade
A to -tal e - clipse_ of the heart_

THE WIND BENEATH MY WINGS

Words and Music by Jeff Silbar and Larry Henley

Bb Bbsus4 Bb Ebadd9 Bb Bbsus4 Bb
13
So I__ was the one with all__ the glo - ry,
2. It might have ap - peared to go__ un - no ticed
while you__ were the one with all__ the
but I've__ got it all here in__ my

Ebadd9 Cm7 Bb/C Cm7 Fsus4 F
16
strength.
heart.
A beau - ti - ful face with-out__ a name, for so long,
I want you to know I know the truth, of course I know it,

Cm7 Bb/C Cm7 Fsus4 F D7/F# Gm Eb
19
a beau - ti - ful smile to hide__ the pain.
I would__ be no - thing with - out you.
Did you ev - er know__ that you're my
Did you ev - er know__ that you're my

Bb F/A Gm F/Eb Bb F D/F#
22
he - ro?
he - ro?
And ev - 'ry-thing I would like to_____ be?__
You're ev - 'ry-thing I wish I could___ be.__

Gm   F/E♭   E♭   B♭   Fadd9/A   Gm7   Cm7   Fsus4   F
I can fly high - er than an ea - gle,______ 'cause you are the wind be - neath my_
1.
B♭   E♭6/9
wings.
2.
B♭   Fadd9/A
wings.
Gm   E♭   B♭   F/A   Gm   F/E♭
Did I ev - er tell you you're my he - ro? You're ev - 'ry - thing, ev - 'ry - thing I wish_ I could
B♭   F   D/F♯   Gm   F/E♭   E♭   B♭   Fadd9/A   Gm7
be.______ Oh__ and I,___ I could fly high - er than an ea - gle;___

for you are the wind be-neath my__ wings.
'cause you are the
wind__________ be - neath my____ wings.__
Oh, the wind_ be - neath my_ wings.______
You, you,_ you, you are the wind be-neath my__ wings.
Fly,_______________
fly,_______________
fly________ a - way,
you let__ me fly__ so__ high.___ Oh___

you, you,___ you,___ the wind be - neath___ my___ wings.________ Oh________
you, you,__ you,__ the wind__ be - neath my__ wings. Fly,______________ fly,__
________________ so high a - gainst the sky,__ so high__ I al - most touched the sky. Thank
__ you,___ thank you, thank God__ for you,__ the wind be - neath my___ wings.

YOU'VE GOT A FRIEND

Words and Music by Carole King

Ab   G7sus4
Close your eyes____ and
Keep your head____ to -

C7   Fm   Caug7   Fm   C7/G   Fm
think of me____ and soon   I____ will be there,____   to
- ge - ther____ and call   my___ name out loud;____

Bbm7   Cm7   Db6/Eb   Eb
bright - en up____   ev - en your dark - est   night. __ }
soon you'll hear____   me___ knock - in' at____   your   door. __ }

Db6/Eb   Ab
You just call____   out my___ name____   and you know

143
23
Db Ab
wher-ev-er I am___ I'll come run-nin'___
26
Db6/Eb
to see you a-gain.___
29
Ab Abmaj7 Db
Win-ter, spring, sum-mer or fall,___ all you have to do is call___
32
1.
To Coda
Ab6 Ab7 Db Cm7 Bbm7 Db6/Eb
and I'll be___ there.___ You've got a friend.

35
Ab Db/Ab Db Ab/C Bbm Ab
38
Gm7 C7 N.C. Db Cm7 Bbm7 Db6/Eb
2.
2.If the sky — there,— yes, I will.__________ Now
41
Gb Dbadd9 Ab
ain't it good to know that you've__ got a friend__ when peo-ple can be__ so cold?__
44
Abmaj7 Db Gb7
— They'll hurt__ you, yes, and de-sert__ you, and
mp

Fm
B♭7
B♭9
B♭m7/E♭
take your soul___ if you let them.
Oh, but don't you let___ them.
Coda
D♭
Cm7
D.S. al Coda
You just call
___ there,___ yes, I will.___
mf
f
B♭m7
D♭6/E♭
A♭
D♭/A♭
___ You've got a friend.___
You've got a
A♭
D♭/A♭
A♭
Repeat x3
friend.___ Ain't it good to know___ you've got a friend.

WITHOUT YOU

Words and Music by Pete Ham and Tom Evans

Slowly ♩ = 60

Cm7♭5
G♭add9
D♭sus4
D♭
shows, yes it shows. _______ 2.No, I
G♭add9
B♭m9
can't for-get ___ to-mor-row when I think of all ___ my sor-row, when I
can't for-get ___ this eve-ning, or your face as you ___ were leav-ing but I
A♭m9
B♭7sus4
B♭7
had you there ___ but then I let you go. And now ___ it's on-
guess that's just ___ the way the sto-ry goes. You al-ways smile
E♭m
E♭m/D♭
A♭7
- ly fair ___ that I ___ should let you know, what you should
___ but in ___ your eyes ___ your sor-row shows, _______ yes, it

To Coda
G♭add9
C♭/D♭
D♭
C♭/D♭
D♭
G♭add9
know.
shows.
I can't live
if
E♭m
A♭m
liv - ing is with - out you.
I can't live,
I can't
A♭m7/D♭
D♭
G♭add9
E♭m
give a - ny - more.
I can't live
if liv-ing is with-out you,
I can't
A♭m
A♭m7/D♭
D.S. al Coda
give,
I can't give a - ny - more.
Well, I

Coda
C♭/D♭
D♭
C♭/D♭
D♭
G♭add9
I can't live___________________________ if
E♭m
A♭m
liv-ing is with-out you,__________ I can't live,____ I can't
A♭m7/D♭
D♭
G♭add9
give a-ny-more.______ I can't live___________________________ if
Repeat and fade out
E♭m
A♭m
A♭m7/D♭
D♭
liv-ing is with-out you,_____ I can't give,__ I can't give a-ny-more. I can't

all woman

All Woman Collection. Vol.1 WITH CD
All Woman Collection. Vol.2 WITH CD
All Woman Collection. Vol.3 WITH CD
All Woman Collection. Vol.4 WITH CD
All Woman. Songbirds WITH CD
All Woman. Power Ballads WITH CD
All Woman. Love Songs WITH CD
All Woman. Jazz WITH CD
All Woman. Blues WITH CD
All Woman. Soul WITH CD
All Woman. Cabaret WITH CD
All Woman Tearjerkers WITH CD
All Woman Bumper Collection WITH CDs

To buy Faber Music publications or to find out about the full range of titles available,
please contact your local music retailer or Faber Music sales enquiries:

Faber Music Ltd, Burnt Mill, Elizabeth Way, Harlow, CM20 2HX England
Tel: +44(0)1279 82 89 82   Fax: +44(0)1279 82 89 83
sales@fabermusic.com   fabermusic.com

YOU'RE THE VOICE

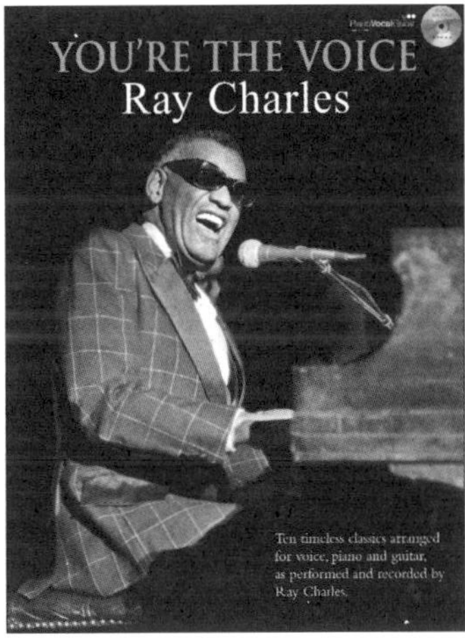

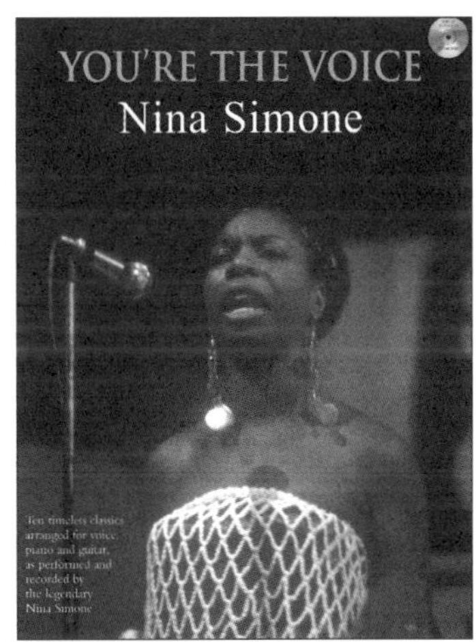

You're the Voice: Shirley Bassey WITH CD

You're the Voice: Maria Callas WITH CD

You're The Voice: Eva Cassidy WITH CD

You're the Voice: Ray Charles WITH CD

You're the Voice: Nat King Cole WITH CD

You're the Voice: Sammy Davis Jr WITH CD

You're the Voice: Celine Dion WITH CD

You're the Voice: Aretha Franklin WITH CD

You're the Voice: Billie Holiday WITH CD

You're the Voice: Norah Jones WITH CD

You're the Voice: Tom Jones WITH CD

You're the Voice: Carole King WITH CD

You're the Voice: George Michael WITH CD

You're the Voice: Dean Martin WITH CD

You're the Voice: Bette Midler WITH CD

You're the Voice: Matt Monro WITH CD

You're the Voice: Nina Simone WITH CD

You're the Voice: Frank Sinatra WITH CD

You're the Voice: Dusty Springfield WITH CD

You're the Voice: Barbra Streisand WITH CD

To buy Faber Music publications or to find out about the full range of titles available,
please contact your local music retailer or Faber Music sales enquiries:

Faber Music Ltd, Burnt Mill, Elizabeth Way, Harlow, CM20 2HX England
Tel: +44(0)1279 82 89 82   Fax: +44(0)1279 82 89 83
sales@fabermusic.com   fabermusic.com

THE
DEFINITIVE
AUDITION
SONGBOOK
TWO CDs INCLUDED
A BUMPER COLLECTION OF 30 ALL-TIME FAVOURITE AUDITION SONGS.
PIANO, VOICE AND GUITAR ARRANGEMENTS WITH FULL LYRICS AND GUITAR CHORD BOXES.
FABER ff MUSIC